The Making of a Winner:

The Porsche 917

The Making of a Winner:

The Porsche 917

by Larry Pihera

J. B. Lippincott Company
Philadelphia and New York

First edition
Printed in the United States of America

U.S. Library of Congress Cataloging in Publication Data

Pihera, Larry, birth date
The making of a winner.

1. Porsche automobile. 2. Le Mans Endurance Race.
3. Automobile racing. I. Title.
TL215.P75P54 796.7'2 72-7354
ISBN-0-397-00807-4

For those who race.
And for those who watch them race.

Contents

Introduction

This is the story of an unforgettable racing car—the Porsche 917. Rough, tough, roaring and snorting, it is a modern car in the grand old tradition of fire-breathing, spine-cracking racers.

When the 917 was first introduced to the high-speed tracks of Europe, it was a loser. In quick time it became known as a killer, a totally unstable vehicle that few men would volunteer to drive. Only a fool or a prophet would have bet that the 917 would go on to win the most prestigious and best-known auto race in the world—The 24 Hours of Le Mans. Only a dreamer could have conceived its transformation into the most successful Porsche of them all.

In 1951 the Porsche organization was a struggling company with few men, few dollars and many dreams. In that year, two cars were hand-crafted in a shed and entered as a "works team" at Le Mans—Porsche's first participation in an international event. Fitted with a small, 1100-cc engine, the surviving Porsche won in its class but did not win the race.

Year after year Porsche teams returned to Le Mans with the same bittersweet results: class-winner, race-loser. The big cars with the snarling engines were the ones that took the winner's laurels. Ferrari, Jaguar and Ford teams considered Le Mans *their* race. They fought and tried to destroy each other and smiled benevolently at the little Porsches. Nice tidy little cars, those Porsches, but certainly not to be taken seriously.

Then the racing scene changed gears. From the dripping forests of Germany came the command: "Design a big car, a winning car."

Dr. Ferry Porsche had issued the order. Designers and craftsmen at the booming Porsche works in Stuttgart had been eagerly awaiting it. With determination born of nineteen years of frustration, they cleared the drawing boards and delivered the blueprints in remarkable time. Everyone agreed: the new car, the 917, would be ready to race in 1969.

After a crash program of ten months, a new racing automobile was ready to assault the tracks of the world. Employing the most modern concepts in automotive design, Porsche engineers fashioned a 560-horsepower flying wedge that could rocket down the straightaways at 230 mph! The brave driver reclined in the cockpit located up front between the wheels.

It was the biggest, loudest, meanest Porsche ever constructed. A challenger? Yes. A winner? Not yet.

There were problems. The 917 had a tendency to veer off the road at high speeds. This made the drivers nervous, to say the least. As a matter of fact, for a while drivers for the 917 were hard to find—a rare thing in racing circles. Normally a racing driver will attach wheels to his fingers, strap an engine to his back and race wherever he is pointed. Seldom is he fazed by anything that rolls.

But such problems were solved with the help of David Yorke of J. W. Automotive, and the 917 began to make its move toward a more promising future.

This is the story of a car that represents the Golden Age of Porsche. It is the story of the only "big car" in Porsche's racing history—a car that could blast all opponents off the track, including the once invincible Ferraris. And it is the story of a car that will no longer be seen racing at Le Mans and similar circuits. The old men who control international sportscar racing have decided to restrict engine capacities for sports cars to 3 litres for the 1972 season. Thus the fire-breathing 4.5-litre 917s that blazed around Le Mans from 1969 through 1971 have vanished.

When those who love racing cars look back at the Porsche 917, they'll see a remarkable automobile that won every race in the Manufacturers' Championship series. A "modern classic," the 917 was faster than any other car Porsche ever built, bigger than any other car Porsche ever built, more successful than any other car Porsche ever built.

This is also the story of a race: The 24 Hours of Le Mans. Colorful, noisy, at times unbelievable, Le Mans is a day-and-nightmare of driving endurance and mechanical durability. Ever popular, invariably spectacular, insidiously perilous. To Stirling Moss, it was the most dangerous race in the world; and World Champion Jim Clark would have nothing to do with it. But for every Moss or Clark there are a hundred others who will risk their lives for the money, for the glory, or simply out of the compulsion to win.

And yet Le Mans is more than a race. It is a carnival. The softest girls, the best food, the worst food, the largest steins of German beer, the most threadbare hippies, Pucci's latest designs in sportswear, the world's most delightful ferris wheel and wild parties—all are part of the glorious tradition that is Le Mans. It is a spirited, emotion-charged event that roars full-bore from Saturday evening until Sunday evening. In the words of one racing enthusiast: "If you haven't been to Le Mans, you haven't seen a race. In fact, you haven't lived."

The Making of a Winner:

The Porsche 917

1 | Le Mans—The Race Begins

June 13, 1970.

The agony of waiting. Fifty-one drivers, strapped into their cars, timebound. Two minutes to go before the rocks in their stomachs dissolve into wet sand. Waiting. . . . Waiting for The 24 Hours of Le Mans to begin. . . . A minute and forty seconds before the green flags turn them loose, blending man and machine in a test of speed and endurance. Waiting. . . . Ninety seconds to contemplate the narrow strip of twisting, turning asphalt that is soon to become their peculiar Main Street devoid of girl friends, wives and children. Waiting. . . . Eighty seconds to try not to think of the unthinkable, to try to forget that steel is hard and flesh is soft. . . . Seventy seconds. Somewhere out there they also wait, a third of a million spectators, watching, waiting. . . .

Le Mans, Grand Prix d'Endurance, race of races.

Dick Attwood feels the tight pull of the shoulder

harness as he shifts his body in the snug cockpit of the Porsche 917. His gloved hands clench the tiny, padded steering wheel. It feels so comfortable now, but later. . . . Sixty seconds. . . . The public address system is blaring. Announcements in English, French and German sound muffled, like the barking of a dog in the distance. Fifty seconds. . . . His eyes conduct a quick muster of the competition: Ferraris, Alfas, Matras and a mix of other makes all lined up at a sharp angle to the pit straight. All are equal now as they wait to leap forward in forty seconds. . . . The Ferraris are out in force: eleven 512s and two 312Ps. Old Enzo Ferrari is not letting up. He never does. Ferraris win at Le Mans. Often. . . . Thirty seconds. . . . Time, money, ingenuity—what more will it take for Porsche to win Le Mans after nineteen years of trying? What more *can* it take? . . . Twenty seconds. . . . Attwood stretches his legs, taps out a tune on the gas pedal to relieve the head-splitting tension. His eyes sweep across the sea of spectators that lap against the trackside barricades. The starters are set. . . . Ten seconds. . . . They are holding the green flags aloft. He watches, swallows, holds his breath and . . . down come the flags, NOW! Attwood hits the accelerator.

The engine of the 917 fires up with a roar. In a smearing blaze of color and ear-splitting noise the cars twist out and head down the Grandstand Straight, sliding through the turn beyond Dunlop Bridge.

Tires leave a trail of blue haze. Dust and stones explode as less tidy drivers dig their rear wheels into the track apron. Cars parry, thrust and wiggle in a reckless effort to gain position. That's what the first lap is all about—position. And that is what makes it so dangerous: the fact that in so short a space and in so short a time all fifty-one drivers are groveling for an objective that is still within everyone's reach. It is here, on the first lap more than any other, that the margin for error is narrowest. It is here that the slightest miscalculation on the part of one driver can knock ten others out of the race. But now the field is beginning to attenuate, and for Attwood, back in the pack, there is one consolation: he can see a bit of asphalt now. He snaps the wooden-knobbed gearshift lever into fifth position, adds weight to the accelerator and feels the 917 respond without a whimper. The speedometer needles 195.

Attwood's body sways to the lateral pull as he maneuvers the machine through the corners. She's holding well, he muses. She can take punishment. There'll be a dice or two with the Ferraris before it's all over, but dammit, she can take it. She's built to take it. But tricky. One small mistake and it's all over. That's how it happened to poor old John Wolfe in practice. One small mistake, and for him it was all over. Forever. Attwood listens to the whine of the engine and frowns. He tries to will the muscles in his neck to relax, aware that he must keep the tension down as long as possible. He has a long way to go. Seemingly longer than the way he has come. . . .

At age thirty he has been racing for ten years. His first campaigner, a modestly powered Triumph, was good to him, and in a year's time he moved into the elite Formula I class. In ten years he has won many races. But never Le Mans.

There is nothing soft, nothing gentle about this course. Already the casualties are beginning to mount. After seven laps Vaccarella has retired his Ferrari, steam billowing from the block. Other disabled cars parked here and there cause the bugs to stir in Attwood's mind. The gearbox, a little too temperamental at times . . . the rims could be sturdier . . . and the brakes more consistent. And the 917, as if resenting this lack of confidence, suddenly cuts its tail loose, forcing Attwood to correct and countercorrect. Yes, she's holding, all right. Man and Porsche are now in ninth place. Only twenty-three hours to go. . . .

Restless, shifting crowds on the safe side of the fence begin to drift from the scene of the race. Surrounding the track are purveyors of a thousand delights. Vendors' booths decorate the grounds like confetti at a wedding. Everything is for sale: food, drink, magazines, programs, racing-team patches, steering wheels, hubcaps and whatnot. Screams can be heard above the rumble of a roller coaster. Young lovers linger outside the "spook house." A barker describes his freak show in exclamatory superlatives.

Mild abandon is the theme of the day, a time for fun and fantasy. But fun takes energy, and energy requires food. There are snack stands that sell spicy French hot dogs encased in small loaves of French bread. There are snack shops selling hot dogs *and* ham sandwiches. And there are deluxe snack shops offering a wide variety of sandwiches as well as those French favorites: hard-boiled eggs. For the knife-and-fork set, there are many full-service restaurants offering complete and even elaborate meals. The more extravagant diners generally select either the sidewalk cafe where they can watch the crowd from bright yellow tables, or an enclosed restaurant where gourmet meals are standard fare.

At Le Mans nobody goes hungry—or thirsty. Coca Cola, America's relief potion for the hot tongues of the world, is sold everywhere. Same familiar script on sign-boards. But: the Coke flavor in France has been altered to suit French palates. It's spicy.

After four and one-half hours Attwood's Porsche buzzes into the yellow pit area, stopping abruptly. He jumps out of the low-slung car. Time for a routine driver change. Attwood's racing partner, Hans Herrmann, snaps on his helmet and climbs aboard the 917. A mechanic slaps the hood: O.K. The 917 spins its wheels, sending up a cloud of acrid smoke, and shoots ahead, the engine squealing louder and louder as the gears are shifted.

Hans Herrmann leans back in the thinly padded seat, extends his arms before him and focuses on the black road that the hungry Porsche is devouring at a remarkable rate. Advertising signs flash past in a kaleidoscope of color. BP. Dunlop. Gulf. Coca Cola.

On the 3.5-mile Mulsanne Straight he jams the accelerator to the floor and revs the engine to the red line. The Porsche twitches its tail but retains a true course. "Easy, my lady. Be faithful. There are many more hours to race."

A popular oasis is the German beer hall behind the pit area. Almost half a city block in size, the vast structure is decorated inside to resemble a mountain-village beer hall. Row after row of raw wood tables stretch across the length of the room. Barmaids in crisp, full dresses swish their hips and petticoats as they scurry back and forth, holding frothy mugs of beer up high, spilling very little.

On an elevated stage, a twelve-piece band featuring an enthusiastic tuba player pumps out a lively succession of back-home-in-Bavaria tunes. Each musician is appropriately attired in lederhosen and a feather-accented green felt hat.

When the sun goes down and the rain falls at Le Mans, the beer hall comes to life. A capacity crowd smiles, sings and sways in time to the oom-pah beat. Frenchmen singing and laughing with Germans. Anything can happen at Le Mans.

The roaring sports cars continue to battle for position, never letting up. In some cars the cockpit temperature climbs above 100 degrees. The drivers endure, determined to finish. Cars coughing, smoking, their fenders streaked with grease and oil, somehow manage to keep going. All for honor, all for reputation. Money is secondary. First place pays less than $13,000, a fraction of what the winner gets at Indianapolis. A single Porsche 917 costs several times the first-place payoff at Le Mans. Obviously, Porsche is racing for something more meaningful than prize money.

The price is high, the risks are great. At Le Mans something "happens" to a car on almost every lap. A driver is killed almost every year. And not even walls can prevent disaster. In 1955 Pierre Levegh lost control of his Mercedes on the Grandstand Straight. The silver car hit the wall, exploded and catapulted into the spectators, killing eighty-three of them and Levegh as well.

Some drivers are "crash-and-burn" types. They are reckless, wild, unprofessional. More often they end up sitting next to a crushed car or lying in a grave than standing in the winner's circle. It is win or nothing with them.

Twenty years of racing attest to the fact that Hans Herrmann is not a crash-and-burn driver. Smooth, precise, careful, he knows the limits of his car as well as he knows its potential. He has combined skill with intelligence to string together an impressive record of wins. He is a quiet man of medium height and cheerful disposition, and when he is not racing he runs a firm known as Auto-Technik in Stuttgart, his hometown. He is forty-two, an old man by racing standards. He plans to retire at the end of the season. A Le Mans victory will make retirement that much sweeter. Many experts consider him to be Germany's greatest sportscar driver. He doesn't want to disappoint them.

The Porsche 917 is the most competitive car he has ever driven. But it is tricky to handle. At times it seems to have a mind of its own. It has an annoying habit of twitching its tail at 195 mph.

It almost always rains during The 24 Hours of Le Mans. This year is no exception. It begins as a trickle and works itself up to a storm. The greasy track seems to become a huge, black, squirming eel, and intermittently the cars behave as if they are being driven by so many drunken drivers.

Dedicated race fans ignore the rain and remain along the Grandstand Straight. These are the ones with oil in their veins. They subscribe to at least three automobile magazines and drive sports cars that they cannot afford. Clever people, they are able to cram two adults and five children into a street Porsche. Quite an achievement. Those who drive Porsche-made cars can recite in litany-fashion every model the company ever made, along with the history of the firm and its racing record. MG owners are equally bright about their cars. Alfa Romeo owners are not so.

The low-slung Porsche 917 roars through the downpour at 230 mph, fenders vibrating from the pelleting of raindrops gone berserk. Misty shapes of cars zoom up from nowhere like attacking sharks. The glorious adventure of Le Mans is now a nightmare out of the darkest pages of Dante. The atmosphere reeks of the raw material of death.

In the parking lot a youth with the features of Michelangelo's David is washing his girl friend's long black hair with beer. He laughs as he watches the foam trickle down her well-shaped T-shirt. He shakes the last drop out of the green bottle and sets it on the ground. Bursting with laughter, the two of them join hands and dance around the bottle in a neopagan revel.

The rain persists as darkness falls, compounding the misery for the drivers. Cars lose shape and form and become bursts of light and sound. Hazy lights from the pits, the restaurants and the entertainment area punctuate the brooding darkness of the unreal, almost mystical world of Le Mans. The ferris wheel glows red and green and yellow as it rotates in the mist. Fragile laughter emanates from unseen clusters of wine-warmed spectators who feel no rain. Throughout this private universe reality has vanished.

Oblivious to the surging crowd of spectators, Herrmann and Attwood contemplate their own reality: Will the torrential rains play havoc with the 917's electrical system? Can the 917 survive the extremely dangerous track conditions without an accident?

Accidents seem to be the order of the day. Four Ferrari 512s eliminated. The unexpected, as always: a slow Ferrari wandering around in Maison Blanche . . . Clay Regazzoni, Derek Bell and Mike Parkes zooming into the corner at 150 mph . . . fiber glass and metal exploding in all directions. Steel guardrails bend like rubber as spinning red Ferraris slam against them again and again. Four of Enzo's dreams ground into scrap. Now only the Ferrari of Jacky Ickx remains in a challenging position.

When the race is nine hours old, a mechanic holds up a chalkboard to notify Hans Herrmann that he is in third place.

Herrmann started racing relatively late in life. At the age of twenty-four he entered his first serious competition, a rally, with a secondhand Porsche. Most racing drivers begin their quest for silver trophies at age eighteen or thereabouts.

Later the same year (1952) Herrmann signed up for his first real race at the famous Nurburgring, where he was fastest in practice in the production sportscar class.

In 1953 he plunged deeply into racing. It was a year of big questions for him. Could he expect good rides? Could he compete with experienced drivers? Could he make a career of racing?

Herrmann tasted the sweet wine of international fame for the first time during this critical year when he drove a Porsche to win the 1500 GT class in the celebrated Mille Miglia.

His questions were being answered—affirmatively. Good rides were being offered. He was competing with and soundly beating experienced drivers. At this point, making racing a career was no longer a question. He was committed.

Tertre Rouge is a tricky corner in the best of weather. In rain it is vile, treacherous—a personal enemy of car and driver—seeking to destroy them on every lap. Humped and arched, short and sharp, Tertre Rouge is a second-gear twist that leads either into a 200-mph straightaway or into the oblivion of a sandbank.

Slicing through sheets of rain, Hans Herrmann buzzes the 917 past the pit area. The car zooms under the Dunlop bridge, through the S-bends and, sliding and skidding with every turn of the wheel, roars into Tertre Rouge.

Judging the moment carefully, the perspiring driver hits the brake and downshifts in rapid succession. The 917's rear end breaks loose. With a deft spin of the wheel, Herrmann brings it under control. Drifting through the corner, the powerful racer is set up perfectly for the straight. He clicks the gearshift lever through third, fourth and into fifth, and pushes the 917 to 195 mph. Again feeling the rear end breaking loose, he eases up on the accelerator. Sliding through a corner is a calculated maneuver. Sliding down a straight is suicide.

A girl with wheat-colored hair is sitting alone at a table at a sidewalk cafe. Pushing an errant lock in place, she stirs her amber drink and begins to read an English-language newspaper.

Before long a Frenchman sits down next to her.

"*Êtes-vous très occupé aujourd'hui?*"

"I'm sorry. I don't speak French. I'm an American teacher. I came to see the race. My cousin was to meet me here, but she became ill. That's why I'm alone, you see."

"*Aujourd'hui je n'ai rien a faire.*" He leans closer to her.

She moves her chair away. "I'm sorry, I just don't understand," she says with a helpless gesture.

Moving his chair closer to her, he looks directly into her eyes and says, "*Les choses qui sont agréables à voir sont belles.*"

"Honestly, I just don't know what you're talking about. I don't speak French. I don't. You're a nice guy, I'm sure. I like your white knit turtleneck sweater. But that's no basis for a relationship, is it?"

Smiling gently, he puts her hand in his and brings it to his lips.

She blushes visibly. "Now that's *very* French."

"*Nous passerons une soirée agréable.*"

"Oh, my. What does that mean?" She leans closer to him. Their noses almost touch. His brown eyes are warm and . . . innocent? His unlined face seems honest. His smile is genuine. True, he isn't shy. Maybe a bit brash. But he does seem gentle enough.

When he puts his arm around her, she decides not to recoil. She relaxes instead. He points to a picture of food in her paper.

"O.K." She nods, smiling her very best smile. After all, it's so important for Americans to make a good impression on foreigners these days.

Approaching Ford Chicane, the 917's lights reveal a scene from a driver's nightmare. A Ferrari is scattered over the road. Men are running back and forth across the track. A red light is flashing.

Ickx is out, Herrmann realizes. Ickx is indeed out, but unhurt. His Ferrari is out, and badly damaged. The racing official who stood where the Ferrari spun is also out—forever.

In a small, dark cabaret in the town of Le Mans, the silence is fractured by a five-piece jazz band. The musicians—products of the Twenties—provide a sound that syncopates with nostalgia. Here the "beautiful people" congregate. Each year they select a new after-dark headquarters. The "beautiful people" are the guys and dolls who smile a lot, wear Pucci-designed clothes and have no financial worries. They appear carefree, happy, friendly and expensively informal. Many of them follow the sportscar carnival from track to track and from continent to continent. Knowing one or two drivers intimately, they form cults to cheer and encourage their favorites. The encouragement includes such fringe benefits as business loans, stock-market tips and warm attention from the female members of the bright and beautiful set.

The walls of the little cabaret are whitewashed. The tables are unpainted. The only illumination is provided by candles jammed in wine bottles on tables. A fine blend of the aromas of dampness and stale wine permeates the room.

No one seems to object to the less-than-deluxe accommodations. Apparently, to the well-heeled visitors, this poor cafe is charming and quaint, an example of the pure, worthy things in life.

In the corner of the room a man leeringly whispers something in his companion's ear. She pretends to be shocked. Then both of them laugh. At the other end of the jazz-filled room, a man in a buccaneer shirt begins to clap in rhythm as his raven-haired partner starts a bizarre bump-and-grind routine.

A portly man with a soiled white apron around his waist waddles over to the jerking performer.

He taps her on the shoulder. "Madam, you must stop."

She keeps right on gyrating along.

"Madam, please."

Gr-r-rind and . . . bump!

"Madam, this is not Paris."

Bump and bump and bumpety-bump!

Rubbing his bald head, he appears puzzled. He runs a respectable establishment. He must act now or one thing will lead to another. He does not want trouble with the police.

In a quick motion he swoops her up over his shoulder, pushes through the crowd and deposits her on the sidewalk. Bump!

"One must be firm," he mumbles as he returns to his position behind the bar.

Another casualty: Jo Siffert has overrevved his Porsche engine. That's it for the Wyer team. At the halfway mark the Herrmann-Attwood Porsche 917 moves up. Streaked with grease and oil, the once-sparkling orange and white 917 now leads the field of fatigued men and machines through the eerie hours of the new day. At 8300 revolutions per minute, the 560-horsepower, air-cooled engine propels the fiber-glassed body around curve after curve. Goodyear tires plus an advanced suspension have kept the 917 on the road while other cars were ramming guardrails and sandbanks.

The sun paints a white glow in the purple sky. Daylight at last, and drivers sigh with relief. Then they see the battered, weatherbeaten wrecks in the first light of day. Cars with blown engines, smoke-stained bodies, crumpled frames, twisted axles, missing wheels, cars that seem held together entirely with silver tape. Discarded toys.

The hours tick away. Drivers sag from exhaustion. Arms, legs, backs, eyes protest the punishment. But it isn't over yet as the men struggle to keep their attention focused on the road. A mental lapse now poses the greatest danger.

In the German parking lot three lovely Teutonic lasses are sitting on top of a Volkswagen camper dangling their legs and waving enthusiastically at passersby. Soon four interested young men are struggling to climb atop the camper. The light rain that is now falling makes it a slippery job. Laughing hysterically, the girls reach down to help—by tugging on shirts and lifting bodies by the ears. The boys finally reach the summit, where they receive a warm welcome. Someone starts to play a harmonica, they dance and for a while the sound of roaring engines seems to subside.

The end is drawing near. Hans Herrmann at the wheel of the 917 is taking nothing for granted. The year before, piloting a 908, he was in first place on the last lap. But Jacky Ickx in a more powerful Ford GT roared ahead and won by a scant 100 yards.

Herrmann is supercautious now. He listens for irregularities. The seven oil pumps must continue to function. The long chrome-nickel steel crankshaft with six journals and eight main bearings mustn't fail now. Each nut and bolt must hold.

Less than one lap to go! Herrmann zooms past a slower car. Arnage Corner ahead! He hits the brake pedal, heel-and-toes down to fourth, third, second. Correcting and countercorrecting, he slides the 917 through the sharp bend. Up through the gears. The fields and faces are a blur. He spots an abandoned car at trackside and is thankful that it didn't happen to him. Look out! Remember that oil patch. Don't spin out now!

He lifts his foot from the accelerator for White House Corner, then jams it down hard for the Grandstand Straight. His heart begins pounding when he buzzes around the corner and sees the bright tall grandstand with its multicolored posters and many flags.

"This is it! I've done it! I've won Le Mans! Porsche has won Le Mans!"

An official slashes the air with a checkered flag. The race is over.

2 | Celebrating the Victory

When Hans Herrmann crossed the finish line at 4:02 on Sunday afternoon, the sky was glowing in a great burst of warm sunlight. The rain had vanished. Golden rays streaked the track and the winning 917 as if in symbolic blessing.

The crowd went wild. Spectators cheered, whistled, screamed, sang, cried, threw hats in the air, and embraced in ecstasy. Porsche had tried and tried to win Le Mans. The little auto maker from Stuttgart finally did it! The underdog had soundly thrashed the giant from Modena. Germans, Frenchmen, Americans and Englishmen all cheered the Porsche team. There was rare unity among nations. Of course the Italians favored Ferrari. But they *had* to. It's a national obligation.

In the midst of the surging, screaming crowd, Herrmann and Attwood hopped on the back of a truck and took a "lap of honor." They were thrilled but absolutely exhausted, their bloodshot eyes sunk in blue circles of fatigue. Exuberant fans used bottles of champagne as spray guns, drenching the victorious drivers.

Along the fence, people were chanting in singsong fashion: "Porsche. Porsche. Porsche."

Some of the more avid fans bolted the fences and ran to the truck in an effort to touch the hero-drivers. Then on the way home they could pretend that the highway was Mulsanne Straight.

More trucks joined the victory caravan. These held Porsche 917 mechanics, other members of the team and Porsche officials. Needless to say, there was much smiling, laughing and back-slapping.

A grease-stained mechanic told a spotless Porsche executive, "I love this 917. I think I'll buy one to drive to work in."

"Where will you get seventy thousand dollars for a 917?"

"My wife can scrub floors for extra money."

Everyone was happy. The scent of victory floated through the air like expensive French perfume.

A sweet young thing with flowing blond hair slipped out of her blouse to do a fiery flamenco victory dance. She stamped out pulsating rhythms as she moved in circles, clapping her hands above her head. A dark-haired boy in jeans accompanied her on his guitar. The pace quickened. The blonde moved with increasing speed, a blur of pink flesh, stamping the ground, throwing her head back, hair flying. The crowd clapped in time to the music. Then someone shouted, "*Gendarme!*" The girl was wrapped in a blanket and whisked away as the police appeared.

An impromptu parade formed in the parking lot. The band consisted of an old-fashioned accordion, a battered trombone, the ever-present guitar and a child's drum. Marching in single file, the out-of-tune musicians soon attracted kindred spirits who hooked on to form a snakelike column. Around the parking lot they marched, singing German songs, jumping over lovers on the grass and dodging departing cars.

An intense young German ran along the Grandstand Straight guardrail, kissing all the girls he could reach until an irate husband chopped him on the back of the neck.

Although the celebrating was charged with twenty years of pent-up emotion, it was short-lived. An hour after the race, the spectators were gone. The grounds were deserted. Food stands were boarded up. Race programs littered the soggy grounds. A tent entrance flapped noisily in the evening breeze. The race was over. The spectacle had ended.

In the early days of Le Mans, ordinary cars that drove on the streets of the world competed in the twenty-four-hour race. If you were wealthy enough, you could buy a duplicate of a winner's car and take your girl for a ride.

After World War II the rules were changed and a new monster was bred. Called "racing sports cars," they were thinly disguised Formula I cars. Because of their superior aerodynamic design, they could snort along the tracks faster than anything else on wheels. But only the rich could afford to own these hand-built sizzlers.

Small, relatively inexpensive cars still race at Le Mans. But they don't win. Most drivers feel that the small cars get in the way. Some drivers consider them a safety hazard. When one car is moving at 230 mph and another is darting about at 90 mph, both cars are in danger of being demolished.

The average spectator drives to Le Mans. Up to a certain point, the journey is extremely pleasant: sun-yellow wheat fields, tall silver-green poplar trees and dull ochre villages dot the route.

But then, for many, the drive turns into an endurance test. Exactly twenty-five miles from the track, traffic becomes a stop-and-start fantasy. Wait for five minutes. Move ahead for ten seconds. Say eighty profane words. It's a supreme test of patience that no one passes with good grades.

During the race itself there is chaos around the track entrance for twenty-four hours. Cars are everywhere, heading in all directions. Swarms of people are coming and going. But it's a happy crowd and it remains happy throughout the hot day, the cold night, the rain, the mud, the dust.

Parking lots are color-coded. If you are rooting for the Italian team, you park in the red lot, since red is Italy's racing color. Favor the English? Park in the green lot. French? The blue lot. A large piece of colored cardboard nailed to a tree identifies each lot.

The parking lots extend as far as the eye can see. For fifty-one weeks of the year most of the lots serve as pastures for animals. On the weekend of the race they become pastures for people. Everyone stakes out six feet of land behind his parked car for breathing space. In this area, deck chairs, sleeping bags, cooking grills and small children are carefully positioned. This six-foot chunk of ground will be home for a family of six for twenty-four hours.

The mad fun began in 1923 when the first 24 Hours of Le Mans was staged. The race is run on roads normally used by regular passenger cars. Unlike participants in the Indianapolis 500, the drivers do not buzz around and around in silly circles. At Le Mans, the perspective is larger. There are left turns, right turns, fast bends, slow bends and a $3\frac{1}{2}$-mile straight that is longer than Indianapolis itself. (The rest of the track covers $4\frac{3}{4}$ miles.)

The race, held in June, always begins on Saturday at 4 P.M. and ends at 4 P.M. on Sunday. When the race is over, the fastest cars have traveled farther than the distance from New York City to Salt Lake City.

Brave drivers with legendary names have raced at Le Mans over the years: Juan Fangio, Carroll Shelby, Stirling Moss, Mike Hawthorn and Phil Hill. They came from all parts of the globe: Argentina, United States, Britain, France, Germany, Australia, Italy, New Zealand, Belgium, Finland. Nobody has achieved more victories than the Belgian Olivier Gendebien, who has taken the checkered flag four times. Just to finish at Le Mans is regarded as remarkable. To win is deemed miraculous.

The town of Le Mans rests on a hill above the River Sarthe, about 130 miles southwest of Paris. An ancient city, it has survived a Roman conquest (58 B.C.) and numerous medieval sieges. The tall ochre Gothic cathedral of Saint Julien stands in the center of the town. On Saturday mornings flower and vegetable vendors display their wares on carts at the foot of the cathedral. Mothers walk with their children through the delightful park and the spirited seek entertainment in the cabarets. With a population of 136,000, four passable hotels and one good restaurant, Le Mans must be considered a family-man's town. Frivolity is present only in modest amounts. Le Mans definitely is not the sin capital of France.

This is the city that attracts over 350,000 persons who spend three million dollars at every Grand Prix d'Endurance. With the exception of Indianapolis, no other city is so completely identified with a racing event that it loses its identity as a commercial entity. For a twenty-four-hour period in any year, Le Mans is the center of the racing world, swarming with excited people. The rest of the year the city doesn't exist for them.

A few days after the Porsche triumph an unprecedented victory celebration was held in Stuttgart, home of Porsche manufacturing operations.

Stuttgart (population 650,000) is a city noted for its industry, culture and green space. Mercedes-Benz is also headquartered here. A center for fine optical equipment and book publishing, it is a city on the move.

Visitors to Stuttgart often exclaim over the cornfield and vineyards that dot the downtown section. These fertile fields represent an integral part of a plan to preserve the natural environment. Germans by tradition and heritage are close to the soil. At one time they worshiped forest gods. Old attitudes linger in the blood. Consequently, Stuttgart is a true garden city. Today, when people in America are pouring concrete everywhere, these lovers of the green have built over only one quarter of the total area of the city! Parks, orchards, dense woods, vineyards and those difficult-to-get-used-to cornfields decorate the remaining portion.

The first page of Stuttgart's history was written in the tenth century. Dukes, barons, knights, fair maids and SS men have walked subsequent pages. It is a town that has known joy and sorrow, pleasure and pain, mourning and celebration.

The people of Stuttgart wanted to celebrate Porsche's victory. After all, Porsche was the hometown team. Civic leaders started writing speeches and organizing a parade. The festivities would be noteworthy. This Le Mans-winning orange-and-white 917 must be honored.

Although Porsche had just delivered the 150,000th

vehicle, the company with a daily capacity of 73 cars and total employment of 3,891 was Germany's smallest automobile manufacturer. However, at this moment the creator of the 917 was the biggest car maker in the world by other standards. The name "Porsche" was on the lips of everyone who knew anything about cars.

The Porsche firm and Porsche cars have, from the very beginning, generated mystical loyalty and devotion. Employees put in extra hours without grumbling. Owners of Porsche street vehicles have formed clubs, staged closed races and published expensive magazines full of pictures of the cars they own and drive. They wave enthusiastically as they pass each other on the highway. And it is rumored that they exchange secret handshakes. Some, said to love their cars more than their families, will undergo great sacrifice to maintain their cars in jet-tuned running order. "The kids can do without shoes for one more month. I want to chrome-plate the engine." It is not uncommon for a Porsche owner to drive 200 miles just to get the oil changed at the Porsche factory.

So the people of Stuttgart and the Porsche enthusiasts were determined to stage a proper celebration for the 917.

And what a celebration it was!

The winning 917 in original racing trim drove through the streets of Stuttgart accompanied by a police escort. The deafening roar of the unmuffled engine reverberated off the modern glass and concrete buildings. But the people—lined six deep on the sidewalks—loved the noise. Noise? This was not noise. This was the sweet sound of victory. It was music exquisitely played by virtuosos of the racetrack.

Proudly the 917 toured the hills of this city set among

the pine forests of Germany. Loud, loving cheers followed the car on its route. Geraniums were plucked from window boxes and showered on the passing champion.

A Le Mans winner is a rare thing. A winner from Stuttgart is rarer still. Porsche's success belonged to everyone in Stuttgart, and the entire town gloried in this internationally visible victory.

The parade halted at the city hall where the Lord Mayor D. Klett greeted the drivers, congratulated them and thanked them "for Stuttgart."

Herrmann ran his hand through his perpetually windblown hair. Attwood smiled his crooked smile and said, "Germans know how to celebrate."

Later the Le Mans-winning 917 was installed in the Porsche museum for posterity.

This rough, tough powerhouse of a racer may be seen by anyone touring the Porsche works. When you visit the museum, wait until no one is looking, then sit in the car. Soon visions of a twisting, turning track and rain and screaming cars will appear before you. And you, too, will be at Le Mans in 1970.

3 | A Winning Year

Le Mans wasn't the only race the 917 won in 1970. That year was a very sweet one for the 917 series of automobiles and for the entire Porsche racing department as well. In 1970 Porsche won the International Manufacturers' Championship for sports cars, soundly beating Ferrari, Matra, Lola, Alfa Romeo and all other challengers. Winning all but one contest in the ten-race series, Porsche destroyed opposition by combining the winning characteristics of speed, endurance and road-hugging ability. The blend was perfect. The reward was a tasty, delicious championship.

It was also the year Porsche became a recognized member of the "big league" in auto racing. No longer would people say "cute little cars." There's nothing little about a 12-cylinder, 600-horsepower brute that reaches speeds of 230 mph. There's nothing little about a firm that wins the Manufacturers' Championship. Furthermore, there's nothing little about a win at Le Mans. In the year 1970, Porsche became a giant.

Most of the races that Porsche won in 1970 were hard-fought battles. Only a few were start-to-finish victory marches. A racing team may prepare their cars with computerlike efficiency and attention to detail, but their work-all-night efforts are often destroyed by that ugly lady Fate. This wicked woman causes experienced drivers to miss shifts; causes axles to break; causes ten-cent hoses to split; causes gas tanks to empty before the scheduled pit stop; and causes tires to go flat. Because of her, racing managers retire and drivers lose their hair and occasionally their lives. Her permanent abode seems to be the racetrack, since, in racing, absolutely nothing is predictable. Even superior vehicles and razor-sharp teams suffer at her mischievous fingers, as we shall see in the following brief summaries of the races that led to the 1970 championship for Porsche. Although Porsche entered the old 908 workhorse in a few of these races, it was the speed and endurance of the 917 that locked up the championship.

Two 917 teams competed to bring the championship home to Porsche in 1970. They were the English Wyer team with key drivers Jo Siffert and Pedro Rodriguez, and the Austrian Salzburg team sparked by Richard Attwood, Vic Elford and Hans Herrmann. Needless to say, competition between the teams and between the drivers developed as the season progressed.

DAYTONA—Jan. 31/Feb. 1. In 1970, Florida enjoyed the distinction of fielding two international sportscar races: The 12 Hours of Sebring and The 24 Hours of Daytona. Daytona was held in January, when most of Europe was frozen hard. Sebring was scheduled for March.

Daytona was going to be a tough race, and everybody

connected with the Porsche racing effort knew it. Porsche had lost the race the previous year. And the pain was still present. This year Porsche was fielding the 917, rumored to be a lethal Ferrari killer. What would happen? The spotlight was on Porsche. And Porsche executives were watching the Wyer team closely. Would the English outfit perform for their German masters? Would they win the Championship *and* Le Mans? The Wyer team had worked miracles for the American Ford people. Would they do as well for the men from the Black Forest? Porsche had made a big investment. They were concerned, to say the least.

Ferrari was making a serious attempt to insure Porsche's defeat. The Italian team arrived with a new 512-S complete with a 5-litre engine, and signed on a trio of drivers that would make any racing-team manager shake with envy. Mario Andretti, Dan Gurney and Jacky Ickx, men feared on any track in any machine, wore the prancing-horse emblem of Enzo Ferrari at Daytona.

During practice these drivers did just what was expected of them. There were sad faces in the Porsche pits when Andretti posted the fastest times in practice. Was this a sign of things to come? The new Ferraris were as remarkably fast as gossip had predicted.

However, Porsche drivers were spurred by the challenge. After the race was an hour old the announcer gave the order: Porsche, Porsche, Ferrari.

But wait. Progress was too smooth. Something had to happen. It did. When the race was two hours old, Fate appeared on the track and touched Jo Siffert's Porsche. Immediately Jo rolled into the pits with a flat tire. Fate has sharp nails. Back on the track, Siffert extended his every ability to work his way past Matras and Ferraris. After an outstanding pursuit he snagged second. The Rodriguez/Kinnunen Porsche was in first. Fate found an engaging playmate in Siffert. He was forced out again. Clutch failure. Mechanics pounced on the 917. Wrenches turned. Nuts flew. The grease-stained mechanics became a little more grease-stained. A stubborn bit of metal was cursed in disciplined German. Pressure was applied. The clutch was ready. Siffert took up the chase once again. Reeling in car after car, he soon gained third position. The Andretti/Ickx Ferrari was in second. A battle began. Siffert pressed the 917's nose to the back of the Ferrari. Around the track the two cars roared at fantastic speeds, dangerously close. Then Siffert outcornered Andretti, grabbing second. Porsches were in first and second. Wait. Andretti passed Siffert. But he couldn't hold it. Siffert squinted, twitched his moustache and moved ahead again. It was a seesaw contest. Just six minutes from the end of the race tiny Siffert made one great lunge, snatching second from the capable Andretti. The Wyer Porsches owned first and second places when the race was over.

SEBRING—Mar. 20/21. This 12-hour race is held on an abandoned airfield in Florida's flatlands. Seemingly located in the middle of nowhere, the track is nevertheless one of America's most popular race circuits. Sebring is almost as mystic as Le Mans to sportscar fans.

Porsche was well represented at Sebring. Two 917s were entered by John Wyer's J. W. Automotive Engineering, Ltd., of Slough, England. The driver teams for these cars were Siffert/Redman and Rodriguez/Kinnunen. Porsche-Salzburg, the team that won at Le

Mans, brought two 917s that were piloted by Elford/Ahrens and Herrmann/Lins. John Wyer, head of the official Porsche factory team, was surprised to see another Porsche factory team. He just shook his head at the inscrutable Germans. "Another blitzkrieg attack," he commented. A variety of smaller 908s were entered by private teams. No one took them seriously because of their tiny 3-litre engines.

Solar Productions, Ltd., a movie company, was the most newsworthy private entrant. Their 908 was to be driven by movie star Steve McQueen and Can-Am ace Peter Revson. Opinion was divided as to whether this was a serious attempt to win the race or just a publicity stunt. Anyone who really knows Steve McQueen will tell you that he is always serious about his racing efforts.

The race began at 10 A.M. After an hour, three Porsches were leading the two fastest Ferraris. Then Lady Fate entered the scene. Suddenly Redman's 917 stopped dead. No electricity. Fate isn't altogether heartless. She allowed the car to roll to a stop near the pits so that the mechanics could reach it. After 9½ minutes of frantically examining the wiring system with everything but a magnifying glass, a sharp-eyed mechanic let out a happy yell. "I've found it! I've found it!" A barely visible wire which was part of the ignition-automatic fire-extinguisher relay had come loose.

The 917 roared back on the track. Fate wasn't finished with the car, however. She would now attempt the bizarre. As Redman was flying down the straight, the large cooling fan broke loose from the engine, soaring 70 feet into the air, looking like a rocket ship heading for the moon. Fortunately, neither cars nor spectators were injured.

Other 917s were eliminated as a result of bad wheel uprights, a collision and an overrevved engine. Fate did her job well. Ferrari triumphed.

The 908 of Steve McQueen and Peter Revson came in second, the highest-placed Porsche. Some show for a movie star who only races on a part-time basis. Now the racing fraternity takes McQueen seriously. Very seriously.

Fourth was the best that a 917 could do. This car claimed the distinction of having three drivers. Rodriguez and Kinnunen were the original drivers, but Siffert took over after his 917 went sour. David Yorke, the Wyer team manager, respected Siffert's calm, yet daring technique at the wheel and used him at every opportunity.

And *that* was the race Porsche lost in 1970.

BRANDS HATCH—Apr. 12. Another month, another race track, another leg of the journey to the championship, and another monumental battle between Porsche, Ferrari and Matra—and between Wyer and Salzburg.

Two days of practice were scheduled for this 1000-km race on a twisty, 2.65-mile track in England. Brands Hatch's many corners have colorful names. Druids Hill Bend, Hawthorn Bend and Dingle Dell are three samples. (Strange how sportscar people consider it important to name every straight, curve and outhouse on the track.) Because of the tight corners, the big sports cars found it difficult to beat the lap times from the previous year. Again and again the drivers strapped on their helmets, snapped on their safety belts and hurled their big 917s and Ferrari 512s around the track in a determined effort to set a new lap record. Perspiration ran. Hands blistered. Just before the end of the practice period Amon in a Ferrari did it. A new lap time was set—1:28.6. The old time of 1:28.8 was equaled by Ickx in a Ferrari and Elford in a 917.

On race day a severe storm pelted the course. Umbrellas and raincoats were the uniform of the day. Mud was everywhere. Originally it was restricted to the parking lot, but running feet carried muck to all parts of the track. A chilly, penetrating dampness compounded the discomfort. A foul day to be a spectator. A depressing day to be a driver.

As the race started, the rain increased. Drivers were virtually blinded by the splash and spray of the cars in front of them. Hanging on to the track became a lost art. Cars slid, spun and drifted in bizarre angles. An unfortunate Lola tried to negotiate a turn backwards with Big Trouble the obvious reward. Like a rubber ball the car bounced off the pit barrier, bounced back and forth across the track and then dug into an earth bank in front of the grandstands. Bits and pieces of the once-lovely Lola were widely distributed.

Vic Elford, driving for the Salzburg team, quickly grabbed the number one spot in a challenging 917. Various Ferraris plus Rodriguez and Siffert in 917s took up the chase. Soon, however, Siffert was out of the contest with a damaged tire. His old friend Fate was still stalking him. In the pits Siffert said to a mechanic, "I'm going to buy a rabbit's foot for luck. On second thought, maybe I should buy a whole rabbit." Increasing the pressure, Rodriguez slid around the track, demanding all that the 917 could deliver. And it delivered in winning measure. Soon Rodriguez swept past Elford, locking up first place. Rodriguez demonstrated outstanding ability as a "rain driver." His speed and control improved as the weather got worse. Dodging spinning cars and abandoned cars, he never eased up on the accelerator. Most drivers slow down during rain. Rodriguez said, "You don't win races by slowing down." The daring driver often told reporters, "You can die crossing the street."

Several Ferraris had dropped out of the race with wet ignition wires. The Porsche 917 proved once again that it is a rain-or-shine winner. Chalk up another victory for the Wyer team and Rodriguez.

MONZA—Apr. 25. This race was held on the famous track on the outskirts of Monza, Italy. Set in a lush, tree-lined park that once belonged to the Italian royal family, Monza draws huge crowds of highly emotional people who have the dangerous habit of running onto the course while the cars are blazing past. These fans cheer, yell, scream and cajole the Ferrari team they dearly love.

Monza is 3.57 miles long and fast and dangerous, and drivers hate it. Slipstreaming is practiced to an excessive degree at Monza, and drivers hate that, too. In slipstreaming, a car will run very close to a car in front of it. The first car cuts through the thick air barrier, pulling along the car behind. The second car gets a free ride, so to speak. By this method a slow car can move faster than normal conditions would permit. By mastering this technique, a driver can pop out of the air pattern and rocket himself in front of the towing car. Races have actually been won in the closing seconds by slipstreaming drivers.

As the racing season progressed, a spirited rivalry was growing between the Salzburg and the Wyer Porsche teams. The Wyer people considered themselves the official Porsche team. Yet it was obvious that the Salzburg team felt that *they* represented the factory on an official basis.

Thus far the Wyer team had snagged all the victories for Porsche. Elford driving for Salzburg was determined to change that. He arrived at Monza with a 4.9 engine in his Porsche. The biggest Porsche engine to date. Bigger than the Wyer engines.

The 917 was in enemy territory at Monza, Ferrari's home track. Few spectators dared cheer for Porsche. Ferrari was eager to win this one for the hometown fans. During that season the Ferrari team had won only the Sebring contest. Ferrari was used to being a winner. At Monza, Ferrari drivers were frenzied men.

The starting flag was waved. A cloud of smoke. The cars roared away. The Elford/Ahrens 917 leaped ahead of the pack on the eleventh lap and led until the ninety-second lap, when a tire exploded on the Curva Grande. The car literally jumped into the air and started on a crazy spin. Ahrens, twisting the steering wheel back and forth, downshifted simultaneously, forestalling what could have been tragic consequences. But the car was out of the race. Elford kicked the side of the pit wall in frustration.

Evil Fate was riding with Siffert again. On the eleventh lap he was forced off the track into the grass as he tried to pass Gerhard Koch's Porsche 908. Koch, concentrating on a difficult stretch of track, had not seen Siffert approach him and inadvertently pulled in front of Siffert at a critical moment. To avoid contact, Siffert deliberately spun his 917, going off the road, tangling the front suspension into spaghetti.

From the ninety-second lap the 917 of Rodriguez/Kinnunen led the chase around Monza. Only twenty-two seconds behind them, Ferraris were constantly snapping at their tires, waiting for a moment of weakness, an error in driving judgment. The finishing order in the 1000-kilometer event was Porsche, Ferrari, Ferrari, Ferrari. Close! But the hard-charging Rodriguez had scored again for Wyer.

The fastest race lap was posted by Elford in a 917. His 1:24.8 beat the old record of 1:25.2, established by a Formula I car, again proving that the 917 was the fastest racing car in the world.

TARGA FLORIO—May 3. Porsche left the 917s back at the factory for this fierce race through the wilds of Sicily. Why? Because the 45-mile Targa Florio circuit has more curves than Raquel Welch. The 11-lap race is all wiggly-jiggly driving. The enormous power of the 917 would be useless here. Weight is important, however. So the 908 was stripped down to a superlight 1,215 pounds. In the race the lead changed time and time again. Porsche was first. Ferrari was first. Porsche. Ferrari. At the end—when first place really matters—the Porsche of the Siffert/Redman team was in the winner's circle. Siffert? Yes. Old Siffert won. Fate must have slept through this race. Or perhaps she found a new favorite.

SPA—May 17. First used in 1925, this 8.76-mile-long circuit is one of the fastest on the schedule of sportscar races. It is one of the few remaining "road-racing" tracks, consisting of real public roads. As a result, telegraph poles, fences, houses, streetlights and trees compound the dangers of high-speed driving. The track abounds in corners, many of which must be taken flat out. Pedro Rodriguez said, "It is a course that fast drivers enjoy." Rodriguez loved it. He loved all dangerous tracks.

Spa is set in a pine-wooded hilly area. Trout streams gurgle through the valleys. Cows graze on the hills, and bright flowers glow in the meadows. The scene of the race is a pastoral delight, an artist's heaven.

The 917, of course, was made for fast courses. The car was a tiger. The big engine, the aerodynamic body and a brave driver were the growl, muscle and fangs of this monster of the raceways. Spa was a tasty track for the 917—one which the car could swallow whole.

The motor meal began during practice. Rodriguez's 917 posted the fastest time—3:19.8. Siffert was next in line with 3:23.9. The best Ferrari could do was 3:30. The crowd looked at the 917 with awe. This was a car that had clearly reached the highest levels of racing. It was rapidly becoming a legend. Spectators wanted to get close to it. Touching it as mechanics worked on it in the paddock area was a supreme thrill, a sensuous experience. Posters depicting the 917 were the hottest-selling items at the amusement booths.

The Salzburg campaigners gritted their teeth. Wyer was taking all the victories. Elford kicked the pit wall. "This is our race!" he fumed. Attwood and Herrmann agreed with him. Extra care was taken to prepare the Salzburg cars on the night before the race.

Siffert of the Wyer team had a different reason for brooding over the way the scene was being cast. He knew that he was as fast as Rodriguez. However, Rodriguez had won three races. Siffert had won one. If it hadn't been for bad luck. . . .

Rodriguez bolted into first position as soon as the race

began. Siffert in his 917 staged a slambang battle with him. Wheel to wheel they roared down the straights, with Siffert dropping behind on the curves. Their personal contest was exciting—and dangerous. Two of the world's fastest and gutsiest drivers in the world's fastest sports cars were staging a man-to-man duel. Siffert wanted this one. He would risk life itself to get it. Sitting low in his 917, he pressed harder and harder on the accelerator.

Out of nowhere Ickx's Ferrari appeared, unexpectedly passing Siffert. A fast and courageous driver, Ickx threw his car around the track in a fierce effort to remain in front of Siffert. He used every trick in the book. However, the 917 passed Ickx on the seventh lap, regaining number two position. There was no holding Siffert back. Obsession had become his invisible copilot. Apparently Lady Fate resented the snub. During Jo Siffert's pit stop she clogged the filler pump, causing him to lose more than half a minute. Maybe now she would leave him alone for a while and go find someone else to bug. Sure enough, she found a new victim in Rodriguez. Poor Pedro lost the lead to Ickx when he was forced to change a cut tire. Then his 917 dropped out of the race for good when Fate caused an electrical failure.

At this point in the race Surtees was piloting Ickx's Ferrari, and Redman was in Siffert's 917. Staging a brilliant demonstration of the technique of sportscar driving at the outer limits, Redman gave the cheering crowd an exhibition of the 917's extraordinary capabilities as he chased and eventually passed Surtees. Never letting up, Redman continued his nerve-racking, tire-screaming, tail-sliding pace and increased his speed with every lap until the checkered flag fell to signal the end of the 1000 kilometers of Spa. Siffert and Redman and their 917 won. Siffert, the Swiss national with the French face, smiled for an entire week.

Motor journalists around the world were beginning to rank the 917 with the great cars of all times. A car that appeared a failure at birth was transforming itself into a consistent winner at maturity. The 917 was chalking up new marks in the record books. It was the fastest and most durable car on the tracks. But the question remained: Could the 917 keep it up? Would Fate step in, causing unusual failures? This had happened before. The sportscar community was watching this unusual car with unusual interest.

NURBURGRING—May 31. The huge 14.2-mile Nurburgring is notorious for its narrow track, twisty configuration and roller-coaster characteristics. It's a track for small, light cars. High speeds are not critical. Therefore the 917s were not selected to carry the Porsche banner in Germany.

But Porsche captured first and second places with the old 908s. Ahrens and Elford drove the number one car while Herrmann and Attwood steered the second-place car. Siffert dropped out. Burned bearings this time. The men from the Salzburg team whipped the men from the Wyer team. There was a pagan display of back-slapping, embracing and champagne-drinking after this one.

"I knew we could beat them!" Elford exclaimed at the victory party.

"All we needed was a good German track," said Herrmann with a wink.

LE MANS—June 13/14. Salzburg beat Wyer and Ferrari again. (see Chapter 1.)

WATKINS GLEN—July 11. The town of Watkins Glen, located in upper New York State, is small and picturesque. The shops are charming, the streets are narrow and the people are friendly to the throngs of invaders in their funny barking cars who disturb their quiet community.

The Watkins Glen course is a track that is both short and fast for a Manufacturers' World Championship race, and drivers enjoy its challenge.

John Wyer entered two 917s for Rodriguez/Kinnunen and Siffert/Redman. Porsche-Salzburg was represented by two 4.9-litre 917s. Attwood/Ahrens were the pilots of one. For the other 917, Porsche had signed up Grand Prix World Champion Denis Hulme, a steady, skilled racer. Vic Elford shared his vehicle.

Porsche 917 teams were represented in abundance. A third team—the Martini Racing Team—was on hand with an older 4.5-litre 917 for Larrousse and van Lennep.

Porsche was determined to win this six-hour race in America. Many Americans buy Porsches. As a matter of fact, the U.S.A. is the biggest car market for Porsche. Owners of street Porsches throng to the races to cheer the big brothers of their little cars. Mr. Porsche didn't want to disappoint his American customers and friends.

Once again the competition was formidable. Ferrari entered two 512s. As always, extremely capable drivers were assigned: Andretti/Giunti and Ickx/Schetty. Additional competition was present in the shape of a Lola T70. Lolas, created, designed and built by Eric Broadley of England, always seem capable of sweeping the endurance sportscar series, but somehow they never quite make it. Simply winning an international event seems difficult for this marque. The cars have great potential, however. Broadley is clever and creative. As a matter of fact, his Lola GT was the ancestor of the great Ford GT that was enormously successful at Le Mans and at every other track around the world. The veteran Jo Bonnier and the youngster Reine Wisell were scheduled to alternate the driving chores of the T70. Fans were watching it with great interest.

Everyone in the Wyer contingent was uptight over this race. The team had not won recently. The loss at Le Mans was especially embarrassing. Porsche had hired Wyer to produce a Le Mans trophy. The "official" factory team had failed. The "underground" factory team had succeeded. David Yorke called a drivers' meeting. He walked into the room, said, "I want to win this one," and walked out. The drivers got the message.

Practice for Watkins Glen became an exercise in pride. A driver would go out to establish what he considered his best time. Then a second driver would chop a tenth of a second off that time. The first driver would get back on the course and better the second driver's time. Then the second driver would jump in his car to try again. This I-can-do-anything-you-can-do attitude resulted in times that were only tenths apart. Eventually Jo Siffert gained the top spot on the grid after a sensational display of driving at the extreme limits of adhesion to the road. Fate was not harassing him.

More than 70,000 spectators saw Mario Andretti take the lead on the first lap of the race. Porsche fans moaned in dismay. Was this a sign of things to come? A Ferrari was always tough competition. Andretti in a Ferrari could cause ulcers in racing managers.

Siffert accepted the challenge. Chopping the edges off corners, he narrowed the distance between the Ferrari and the 917.

Siffert used every trick accumulated in years of racing motorcycles, Formula I cars and sports cars and flew after Andretti in relentless pursuit. The 917 seemed as determined as its driver. Without complaint, the big Porsche snapped around the track. Thriving on the stress of minor off-track excursions into the cinders, stones and dust of the apron, the 917 narrowed the distance between it and the Ferrari until, on lap four, the Ferrari was no longer number one.

Siffert was not allowed to relax. Rodriguez, also in a 917, passed Andretti and was roaring after Siffert. Intolerant of any interference, the Mexican bumped slower cars to the side of the track. Second position was an abomination to Rodriguez. First was the only honorable spot. He was an all-or-nothing-at-all driver. Rodriguez inched closer and closer to Siffert, finally overtaking him to begin one of the most spectacular duels in sportscar racing.

Two of the world's greatest sportscar pilots driving identical Porsche 917s for the same team turned a twenty-five-car race into a two-man show. The lead shifted back and forth many times. Siffert. Rodriguez. Siffert. Rodriguez. Maximum speeds were attained. Clouds of dust arose as tires slipped off the track. The 917s wiggled their tails as they took corners unevenly. David Yorke, the Wyer team's racing manager, was in agony. He couldn't convince his drivers to smother their competitive urge. He wanted his drivers to destroy the opposition—the Ferraris and the Lola—not each other. He knew what would eventually happen. And on lap 80 it did happen. Rodriguez and Siffert touched 917s at high speed. Fiber glass flew in all directions. Tires screamed. The cars twisted and turned in a desperate automotive ballet. Both cars staggered into the pits. David Yorke was not happy. His eyes fired sparks. His mouth produced an X-rated barrage of words. And his mechanics went to work.

Soon Rodriguez was back on the track. The damage on his car had been limited to an easily repairable right door.

Fate had dealt Siffert a stiffer blow. His 917 suffered a broken oil-catch tank and tire damage. Thanks to the remarkable efforts of the Wyer pit crew, he was back on the track in record time.

Siffert knew, believed, felt, was absolutely certain that he was faster than Rodriguez. And he was determined to prove it. His 917 performed incredible tricks as he shortened the distance between Rodriguez and himself. Sliding far down in the seat, he entrusted the preservation of his thin, small-boned body to the road-holding abilities of his 917.

Seeing Siffert gain on him, the devout Rodriguez must have prayed: "Dear God, I want to win this one."

The Rodriguez/Kinnunen 917 was in first place when the checkered flag was waved. Number-two spot was secured by the Siffert/Redman 917. The Salzburg 917 of Elford/Hulme finished fourth. The Ferrari of Andretti/Giunti buzzed home in third place. The Lola proved to be less of a challenge than the experts had feared, coming in eighth.

All 917s finished this race, proving once again that they were exceptional racing cars.

AUSTRIARING—Oct. 11. It was Porsche versus Ferrari and Alfa Romeo at the 3.37-mile Austriaring, the last race of the year. A Lola T210 was entered but was not considered a serious threat.

A new circuit, the Austriaring (as the name suggests) is located in Austria in the pine-covered mountains of Styria in delightful country near Zeltweg. But then, where in Austria is the countryside less than delightful? The mountains, the clear air, the pine trees and the friendly, efficient people with their hearty laughter make racing here a pleasure for spectators, teams and drivers alike. Everyone has a good time at Austriaring.

The smooth, well-cared-for track consists of two long sweeping straights with a half-circle turn on one end and a snakelike section on the other.

All corners require a tire-squealing speed of 100 mph to remain competitive. Drivers cannot nap on this circuit.

Alfa Romeo appeared with four cars. Alfa engineers had squeezed 430 hp out of old 3-litre engines and had reduced total body weight to 1,370 pounds. "Watch them," was the word around the pits.

Ferrari had a new racing manager (Dr. Schetty), new horsepower (620) and new streamlined bodies. "Watch them, too," somebody from Porsche said. "Are we going to race or watch?" asked a driver.

In practice, Rodriguez's 917 was fastest with a speed of 1:40.48. Ickx's Ferrari was a hairline away with 1:40.75. Siffert couldn't convince his car to fly. So he settled for the second row on the grid. Rodriguez smiled his boyish smile when he heard of Siffert's position. But he said nothing.

The starting flag fell to signal the beginning of the six-hour race. Ickx shot into the lead. Rodriguez—as was his custom—pushed hard for first, but his 917 slowed to a stop with engine failure in the fifth lap, never having caught Ickx. He shot a dark look of Latin hatred at the 917 as he walked away from it. "Disloyal beast" he muttered.

Siffert, squinting in hard concentration, roared around the track in a tight line without closing on the Ferrari. His team manager wore a black expression. Gulf-Wyer-Porsche-917 personnel had become possessive of first place. They regarded it as their exclusive territory.

The Salzburg 917 team of Elford and Attwood was closing on the Ferrari. Their stomachs were tight with the desire to beat Wyer. And they were on the way, when a stone punctured the oil cooler. The 917 sputtered into the pits for seventeen minutes of first-aid treatment. It was no longer a contender. Elford kicked the pit wall in disgust. A mechanic said, "You're going to have a short foot if you keep that up."

At this point Fate did Siffert a favor. The leading Ferrari's electrical system shut down. Silently the big red car rolled to a stop. Then the Ahrens/Marko 917 that had inherited first place from the Ferrari ran out of gas. Next in line for first place was the Siffert/Redman 917.

But being a decidedly liberated woman, Fate resented being taken for granted. She decided to teach him a lesson. Stirring around in his engine, she caused it to pop and sputter. Not content to stop there, she kicked his transmission, leaving him with one gear—fourth. Perhaps he would respect her now.

Despite this onslaught, Siffert still finished in first place, barely edging a charging Alfa. A Wyer car had won again. Siffert smiled that confident French lover's smile of his as he savored the thought of beating Rodriguez.

The International Championship for sports cars was

complete. Of the ten-race series, Porsche had won nine—an enviable record. The 917 had been entered in eight races, winning seven, including the greatest race of them all—Le Mans.

Two teams masterminded the string of victories. John Wyer of J. W. Automotive Engineering, Ltd., Slough, England, and his racing manager, David Yorke, headed the Gulf-Porsche factory-backed team of Rodriguez-Kinnunen-Siffert-Redman. Porsche-Salzburg, the Austrian branch of the family-owned Porsche business, sponsored the cars of Herrmann-Attwood-Elford-Hulme-Ahrens. The Wyer team won more races than the Salzburg team, but Salzburg captured the big prize—Le Mans.

The rough-and-tumble 917 had justified its existence. It had beaten the best cars of the world in the greatest endurance races of our time. The Porsche 917 coupe built for long-distance racing was indeed a brilliant automobile.

4 | The Very Beginning

The heritage of the stern, unforgiving Porsche 917 can be traced to another century, another country, another culture.

Ferdinand Porsche, founder of the Porsche works, was born on September 3, 1875, in Maffersdorf, a tiny village deep in the Hansel and Gretel forests of Bohemia. It was a fairy-tale world, complete with castles, waltzes and an emperor with a penchant for Gilbert and Sullivan soldier suits. It was an unreal world.

The common man in the hills and the forests of this part of the globe still had a medieval outlook on life: you remained in your station and respected your betters, and you distrusted anything new that threatened to alter the pattern of your existence. When the invention of the first practical typewriter opened new career opportunities for women, the good men in lederhosen thought their sex lives would end. "The infernal clacking machine will drain the passion from women through their fingertips!" New discoveries, such as the telegraph and the electric light, were considered the contrivances of madmen and witches. It was a confused world on the eve of the dawning of a new age.

It was this world that intruded into the life and household of Anton Porsche, a tinsmith who had established a small business to support his family. Anton wanted his son Ferdinand to become a tinsmith so he could take over the family business some day. But Ferdinand had other ideas: he wanted to study electricity. He tried to make his father understand: "Science is the field of the future."

"The future?" Anton boomed. "If you don't learn a trade, you'll have no future. How do you propose to make electricity? From bats' wings and porridge? Do you think you are a witch?"

"I will make electricity from batteries."

"Devil's work. A tinsmith does honest work. And so will you. You are fifteen years old. Too old for play. Electricity. I'll be the laughing stock of Maffersdorf. Me, the vice-mayor. Enough. I have decided. You will work twelve hours a day. Perhaps fatigue will drive this electricity nonsense from your head."

And so, young Ferdinand went to work in his father's shop. But nothing could drive "this electricity nonsense" from his head. He quietly moved his books and materials to the loft over the house, and it was there that he studied and tinkered every day after his father released him from his chores. Of course, his mother knew of his miniature Frankenstein laboratory, but she never mentioned it to Anton.

One day a search for an ax handle led Anton to the loft. When he discovered the laboratory, he flew into a rage and began smashing the equipment, overturning a container of battery acid in the process. The acid ate through his pants, ruined his shiny new boots and caused serious skin burns.

Enough was enough. Something would have to be done. A family council was called. After lengthy arguments, some screaming and a bit of pouting, father and son declared a truce. Ferdinand would be allowed to attend evening classes at the technical institute in Reichenberg. Of course, he would still have to work in the shop during the day.

One evening when Anton was returning home after a long day at the shop, he rounded the corner and stopped dead in his tracks. Good God! The house was on fire! But wait—the glow was even, and there was no smoke. He ran the remaining steps to the house.

The house was ablaze all right—with electricity. Ferdinand, in his dark lab, had conjured a generator, switchboard, incandescent lighting, door chimes and an intercom system. All of this was now installed in his father's house.

Anton stood with his eyes and mouth wide open, no longer doubting that he had a truly gifted son. Shortly thereafter Ferdinand, with his father's approval, left to find work in Vienna.

The difficulties in young Porsche's life weren't over, however. Because his grades at the technical institute weren't high enough, he was denied registration by the officials of the university. As a result he was never graduated from any university or school of higher learning.

He took a job sweeping floors at the United Electrical Company in Vienna. Not exactly a scientific calling. But a job. When university officials again refused him registration, he began sneaking into lectures. When they threw him out, he snuck back in. Again and again and again until at last the university gave up and he was allowed to remain in the lecture theaters.

At the electric company he was promoted to the design office. In 1898 a golden opportunity appeared on the horizon, and Porsche's career began to shine.

Jakob Lohner, coachbuilder to the emperor, decided that horses would soon become obsolete. The automobile was the transportation mode of the future. And batteries were obviously superior to the foul, popping, chugging, hissing, greasy internal-combustion engine.

Lohner wanted a designer with a wealth of electrical knowledge, someone who was young progressive, innovative, original, tireless, persistent. Porsche was hired. He was twenty-three years old.

He was in a dream world. Better still, he could turn his dreams into reality.

He spent great sums of company money on testing equipment and on the construction of prototypes. Transmissions, gears, driveshafts and batteries were shifted here and there with the flash of an idea.

"This may be better," he often said as he set about bringing his latest brainstorms to physical reality. Lohner would examine purchase order after purchase order and mop the perspiration from his brow. "Don't worry," Porsche reassured him, "the proper solution requires experimentation. And experiments cost money. Surely you want the proper solution." More purchase orders were issued.

Work to Ferdinand Porsche was the reason for existence. He was not a social person. Idle chatter bored him. He lived to solve engineering problems, in a unique and individual style. Slipshod work by a subordinate on one of his projects would send him into a volcanic rage. Firm belief in his own ideas would spur him to do battle with anyone who opposed him—no matter the title or position.

Meals were a nuisance. He always carried a hard, dry roll in his pocket. When a lengthy or pressing engineering problem arose, he would not waste the time it took to go out for a restaurant meal. The roll simplified his life.

Family obligations were occasionally overlooked due to pressing business problems. His son was born while he was miles away watching a race. The price of genius is high.

Porsche first stepped into the international spotlight at the World Exhibition in Paris in 1900. The Lohner-Porsche electric car represented Austria in that show. Immediately the individualistic design astonished experts around the world and attracted potential customers.

Typically, Porsche did things his way when he designed the car. This was the first car to be built without a transmission. To achieve this he placed the electric motors in the hubs of the front wheels, automatically providing a front-wheel drive. The total weight of the car was 2160 pounds. Wheel-motor combinations weighed 253 pounds. Moving at a top speed of 37 mph, the car was remarkably fast for the year 1900. After demonstrating the car on a run from Versailles to Paris and back, his car was awarded a grand prize.

Porsche's next design was a mixed-drive vehicle. Batteries were discarded. A gas engine drove a generator which in turn fed energy to the wheel-hub electric motors. The car was new, different, efficient and successful.

In 1902 Porsche was called to active military service for a short time as a private in the Austrian army. True to military mentality, the brilliant automotive engineer was not given an engineering assignment. He was given an automotive job, however. He was made a chauffeur —for the Archduke Franz Ferdinand. The vehicle he drove? The mixed-drive Porsche.

The mixed-drive car proved to be popular everywhere. It sold well. And Lohner was happy. Too happy for Ferdinand Porsche, who was once again a civilian. Lohner refused to allocate funds for Porsche's many new experiments and projects. Lohner said, "Ferdinand, rest, relax. Don't work so hard. Save my money." Porsche insisted upon the validity of his experiments. They parted company.

In 1906 Porsche joined Austro-Daimler, Austria's biggest auto firm. He designed cars for street and track—always emphasizing speed, reliability and durability. These characteristics became the Porsche trademark through the years, reaching a point of refinement in the 917 racing car.

During World War I, Porsche designed motorized carriages to pull 305-mm and 420-mm mortars weighing up to 26 tons. Needless to say, these big bangers did nasty things to human flesh. Porsche did not enjoy being part of the cruelty. He was anxious to return to the peaceful design of racing cars. If a racing driver died, it was a consequence of the driver's choice of profession. In a war too many persons die due to the decisions of glory seekers who sit in comfortable quarters far away from the front. These men say brave things such as "Attack" and "Draft more boys" while they check monstrous casualty reports over martinis. Porsche considered war a waste.

After the war directors of Austro-Daimler screamed for cuts in the development budget. Porsche screamed back, threw a table lighter at one of the directors during a meeting and quit his job as general manager.

In 1923 he moved to Daimler in Stuttgart, where much of his energy and time were devoted to reshaping the company's racing machines.

As technical director, he worked there for more than five years. His designs won the Targa Florio, and several grand-prix races. Again Porsche's opponents moved into positions of power, consolidating their forces against him. He quit.

With the title of chief engineer in 1929, he moved to the Steyr factory in Austria. Almost immediately the Great Depression blew the business world flat. When the dust cleared, Porsche found Steyr had been absorbed by Daimler-Benz. He resigned.

To add depth and meaning to his design life and to avoid the constant quarreling with superiors, he decided to open his own design office in Stuttgart and hired several engineers.

Porsche's reputation had swept across Europe. Business was brisk at first, but the sagging economy brought lean periods. Porsche borrowed on his insurance policy to pay salaries. About his own future he was an optimistic fatalist. "That will work itself out," he said.

During one of the lean periods, Stalin sent his emissaries to offer Porsche the position of "State Designer of Russia." That vast country needed power stations, turbines, trucks and aircraft. At this point in his career, Porsche was intensely interested in developing a small car, a people's car. He was also interested in pushing sports cars to the limits of technical excellence. Russia was not ready for a "people's car." Racing cars? Russia needed bread, not sport. Moreover, Porsche preferred

Pilsner beer to vodka. He decided to stay in Stuttgart.

Eventually business volume increased. His company designed the celebrated Auto Union rear-engine grand-prix racing car, and a record-breaking speed car.

In 1933 Adolf Hitler came to power. His love of cars is not as well known, perhaps, as his fondness for gas chambers and ovens. Almost every month he commissioned a new bulletproof limousine for which he offered design suggestions.

Hitler believed that through cars, racing and super-highways he could buy the loyalty of the people. He began subsidizing Mercedes-Benz and Auto Union on the Grand Prix circuit. He also issued instructions that German cars should hold the land-speed records. And so, in October, 1937, an Auto Union touched 251.2 mph, establishing a new flying 5-kilometer mark.

Shortly after he assumed power, Der Führer summoned Porsche, instructing him to produce a "people's car that would sell at 1000 marks [$240] and possess an economical fuel consumption rate."

Porsche was given a generous retainer by the state. It was all-systems-go for one of Ferdinand Porsche's pet projects.

Thus, the "people's car," grandfather of the Volkswagen, was conceived and born.

Hitler, in his usual ultradramatic style, instructed SS men to road-test the car, making it the first automobile ever road-tested by government security agents.

Porsche, who had little interest in politics, was not a disciple of Hitler. But at this point in time he would have bargained with the devil to bring his small car to life. The development of a car requires vast sums of money. Hitler was the demon with the money. To Porsche, the horns and the tail didn't matter where automobiles were concerned.

No one ever intimidated Porsche. He always had complete confidence in his ideas, beliefs and position. To him, Hitler was just another man, and not a very bright one at that. The fact that Hitler could send those who displeased him to their deaths with a simple flick of the wrist never concerned Porsche. Of course, it should have. As brilliant an engineer as he was, when it came to politics and history, Porsche was not very astute.

During one of the first meetings between the two men, Hitler denied Porsche's request without listening to the prepared argument. Guards began to usher Porsche towards the door. Porsche pulled loose, swung around, stamped across the large room, stopped in front of Hitler's desk, pulled his head into his shoulders and exploded.

"Herr Hitler. I've spent a lot of time preparing this material and I want you to listen."

"See here, Porsche," Hitler interrupted.

Porsche pulled a sheaf of papers from his briefcase, throwing them on Hitler's desk. "Look at these! You'll see what I mean about technical excellence."

Hitler waved away the charging guards, but one of Porsche's men tugged at his sleeve in an attempt to urge him out before it was too late.

Porsche turned on the man, yelling, "Stop that. I must talk with Herr Hitler."

And he talked and he talked and he talked.

Hitler couldn't believe this amazing display of audacity. He just stared as Porsche exclaimed, pointed to papers, gestured or just screamed. But Hitler was evidently impressed with Porsche's knowledge. When

Porsche finished talking, Hitler, only vaguely understanding the technical argument, shook his head and said, "You're right. You're right. I agree."

Although the Hitler-Porsche relationship was amiable enough, Hitler expressed irritation at Porsche's habit of calling him "Herr Hitler." More illustrious titles were available. Furthermore, Porsche discussed all problems with his hands in his pockets. This also disturbed Hitler. "Doesn't he know who I am?" Hitler raged after a meeting with Porsche.

His aide assured him, "That man is eccentric. A genius."

Pounding the desk, Hitler yelled, "A genius can show respect! He calls me 'Herr Hitler.' He stands before me slouched over! Me, Führer of the Third Reich! What is wrong with that man?"

The uniformed aide tried to placate him. "He doesn't mean anything disrespectful by his attitude. It is just his way."

Hitler waved a hand in the air and said mockingly, "His way, his way." He shrugged. "Unfortunately we need his ideas."

Factories were constructed in which the Volkswagen would be produced. Workers were hired. Everything was ready for Porsche's dream car.

Then the bombs dropped and the bullets flew and the world found itself immersed in the monumental blood bath known as World War II. Hitler no longer needed cars to consolidate his position with the little people of his country. He needed guns and bullets to attack the little people of other countries.

So much for Porsche's dream car.

In June, 1945, Porsche was captured by the Americans and imprisoned in a castle. After a few weeks he was released, judged politically neutral.

Then France's minister for industry lured him to French Headquarters at Baden Baden with the suggestion that he resume dreaming about—and designing—his "people's car"—this time for the French.

The French political scene—always a bubbling pot—boiled over. Outside competition was one thing French businessmen did not savor. Especially from a German. Certain influential persons fumed and demanded his arrest. Porsche and his son Ferry were carted off to Paris, paraded in chains through the streets of Dijon and then locked in an unheated cell.

Subsequently moved to the porter's lodge of the Renault villa, Porsche labored over plans for the French small car and supplied French engineers with a steady stream of ideas and improvements. In short order the Renault 4CV was developed. This car proved to be the cornerstone of the postwar auto industry in France.

Not considered as valuable as his father, Ferry Porsche was released from prison to return home, where he divided his efforts between reviving the family business and raising the one million francs demanded by the French for his father's release. Eventually Ferry accumulated the money, paid it, and his father was also allowed to return home.

Dr. Porsche's daughter Louise subsequently married Anton Piech, who had been imprisoned in France with the Porsches.

Ferry and his former associates completed the first car with the Porsche name in May, 1948. Immediately orders began to fill the files. Virtually handmade, this tough little car was the direct ancestor of the great 917 and the beginning of a long line of remarkable automobiles.

Ferdinand Porsche died in 1951. A man whose line of direction in life was firm, who searched for engineering perfection, who climbed to the highest success levels, Porsche held the respect and awe of men engaged in designing automobiles—regardless of nationality or politics.

Before he died, the man who had once been rejected by the university received honorary doctor's degrees from two major universities. Porsche had managed to "graduate" after all. But that was after he had already illuminated the world in his own peculiar fashion.

5 | *The Road to the 917*

A car that wins race after race in seemingly endless succession is not a parentless product. It must, by nature, possess a remarkable genealogy. The tough, dependable and not-too-lovely 917 is the end result of a long line of tough, dependable and not-too-lovely Porsche products for street and track.

Since the first Porsche was completed in 1948, the marque has risen to a position of eminence in the automotive world. In the postwar period many new names have appeared in the world of cars. And disappeared. It's a fickle business. But Porsche's position grows increasingly strong and stable.

Porsche began manufacturing cars in Gmund, Austria—a rather small town somewhat hidden among tall, dripping fir trees and tall, brooding mountains. This isolated community didn't even have a railroad.

The war was over. In this mountain town one could almost believe the earth had never been torn and scorched. Almost.

A carefree, beerhall atmosphere was returning. Laughter echoed through the hills. And girls were eager to be pinched. The Gestapo was gone.

However, in those postwar days in that faraway town, Porsche had problems. The decision to manufacture cars was made under conditions that would make saints swear. Old Dr. Porsche was gravely ill. His son Ferry was doing the work of ten men. The old workshop and offices in Stuttgart were occupied by the U.S. Army. Company personnel were barred from trespassing on the premises. As a result, records could not be checked. Past research had to be repeated. There were shortages and legal restrictions. Parts for the manufacturing of the new automobiles posed a monumental problem. For all practical purposes nothing was available in Gmund. Nothing. Hidden from snooping officials, this idyllic community was a living photograph torn from a picture book of the happy, old prewar world. But its very attributes were obstacles to efficient mass production in the twentieth century. A modern automobile simply could not be produced from pine cones and cuckoo clocks.

Skilled workers were difficult to locate. Mountain climbers and skiers, yes. Mechanics, no. Procuring simple items represented head-splitting problems. For example, Bosch sparkplugs from Germany were considered necessary for the new car. Legally they could not be imported. What to do? A worker had the answer. He would travel to Germany, obtain the plugs, put them in his pockets and walk across the border with his fingers crossed. It worked! And it worked again and again. After a while he had trouble uncrossing his fingers.

Coincidentally, the German army had abandoned scores of Volkswagens and Kubelwagens in this part of Austria during their retreat. These parts were salvaged for the new Porsche car. Porsche employees were often seen wandering through the forests looking for these cars.

In March, 1948, the first car bearing the Porsche name was completed. It was an open car with a 1131-cc Volkswagen engine, and Volkswagen springing, steering and gearbox. In fact, it could be considered a Super VW. Weighing in at 1340 pounds, it was frisky and fast. With an engine tweaked to produce 40 bhp, the car had a highly favorable power/weight ratio. It moved. Hitler would have been proud of it.

The car immediately created a whirlwind in auto circles. The Porsche name had a magic ring. Many customers placed orders for that bit of magic. However, even good news brought difficulties in tow. The international scene was as confounding as ever. Import licenses and currency-exchange tangles involved miles of red tape and interminable conversations with petty bureaucrats whose skills lay in sharpening pencils, not forming decisions. Customers suggested extraordinary solutions. The Portuguese even offered to pay in sardines!

The original car was sold in September, 1948, to a Swiss buyer for 7000 francs. Foreign currency was urgently needed to purchase parts. Without parts there would be no new cars. There was not one remaining Nazi vehicle to cannibalize. New parts *had* to be purchased.

In the early days all body work was hand-formed by one man who was a genius in his field. All the cars were original works of art—true metal sculpture. The curves in the fenders were perfect; the surfaces glistened. But the sculptor had a problem: alcohol. Every so often he took a day off to celebrate some personal holiday, such as his birthday. On such days the Porsche production line also took a holiday. This man actually controlled car output. "Don't worry," he would say when he sobered up, "I'll work around the clock to make it up." And this honest man did. But his unpredictable working habits almost gave Porsche executives ulcers. When an important customer demanded his car, they couldn't very well explain: "You'll have to wait another week. Our body man is still drunk."

Parts and people not withstanding, Porsche prospered. Soon 300 persons were employed in the sticks-and-Scotch-tape operation in Gmund. A coupe was designed and built. It received an enthusiastic welcome from the press and the public. A lightweight drophead version became available through a Swiss connection. Brochures were printed in several languages. At last business gears were moving smoothly.

With maximum production in Gmund limited to five cars a month, a decision was made to move operations to Stuttgart. The first cars produced in Germany were constructed in the Porsche family garage. Soon the production department moved to the Reutter yards. Reutter—the new source for Porsche bodies—had leased 500 square meters to Porsche. In 1956 the old Porsche factory in Stuttgart was finally returned. The Porsche Company no longer was a ricky-ticky group of frenzied automotive enthusiasts. It was now a multimillion-dollar firm employing frenzied automotive enthusiasts. The ride on the golden carousel had begun.

Porsche vehicles developed their own brand of folklore. Strange tales drifted from the forests of Germany. It was said that the cars were made by dwarfs retired from the Snow White villa; that the potential customer had to pass a special driver's test or a car wouldn't be sold to him; that the little cars could drive right through the side of a General Sherman tank and emerge without a dent.

People believed in Porsche.

Just as Porsche believes in Porsche. The Porsche firm is an unusual operation with an unusual emphasis. Sales are important. Production is important. But quality is most important. A car bearing the Porsche name must be distinctive, different, superior. The company officers insist on the development of tough, durable engines, brakes that truly stop the car, components that do not fail at critical times, chassis that are firm, safe, and body styles that are timeless. The Porsche car must not be a source of worry and concern to its owner. It should be fun to drive. Exciting. After all, driving a car is one of the pleasures of life.

The quality of the cars is more than a matter of good business. It is a matter of family pride. The Porsche firm is still family-owned, with various members of the family actively engaged in operating the business.

Dr. Porsche's son Ferry is the managing director. The old doctor's daughter Louise runs Porsche Konstruktionen in Salzburg. Ferry's sons Ferdinand, Gerd, Hans-Peter and Wolfgang head divisions. Each of these younger members of the family gravitated to divisions in which they had an aptitude. For example, Ferdinand III is style-oriented, with a concern for line, shape and form in automobiles. It was natural for him to work in and eventually head the styling division.

The Porsche reputation has been shaped by a comprehensive racing program and by a remarkable production line.

Weak elements readily become apparent during the

long, grueling hours on the racetrack. Developments must come rapidly if a model is to become a winner.

Porsche production cars are manufactured with, as one company official said, "the personal touch." The cars are watched over, assembled, polished and pampered by some of the most skilled craftsmen in Europe.

Exactitude is carried to the highest degree. Every cylinder head is precisely litred out by women workers who are selected for their delicate fingers and infinite patience. Many exotic adjustments are made out of a compulsive attitude that a Porsche must be better. The generator is balanced with the fan wheel to achieve a quiet movement. When the average car maker says, "Forget it, who will know?" Porsche executives say, "This is not tolerable. Change it. Improve it!"

Every engine (not the tenth or two hundredth) is tested at various RPM and HP outputs in the dynamometer room.

In fact, the plant seems to be crawling with inspectors. They are everywhere, checking everything—doors, unwanted air passages, undercoating, welding—everything. Every fifth man performs some sort of inspection duty.

Every car is washed and sprayed under pressure to check the watertight characteristics. Those who have driven leaky cars during a rainstorm realize how important this is. The floorboards of a Porsche don't become footbaths during a shower.

Of course every car is road-tested before it is delivered. The man who tests it is a stern judge. This car reflects upon *his* integrity, you know. It must be impeccable. It must be swift, silent and agile. It is a Porsche.

Porsche's success in racing was an immediate thing.

With inspired power-weight ratios and superb road-holding qualities the cars were first unbeatable in their class—and later unbeatable in any class.

The design road to the 917 was direct if not swift. Improvement followed improvement. Mistakes in design and materials were few. All cars were either rear- or mid-engine vehicles for two compatible reasons: superior road-holding and company tradition.

In America the restless spirit of the pioneer calls for a constant cycle of change. This demand permeates the American life style. Everything changes. And often. Clothing styles, the car, the television, the house, the wife. A definite psycho-economic difference exists between the people who live on the two continents. The difference spreads to the types of cars produced by these varying personalities. On one side of the ocean production cars are made to last decades. On the other side of the ocean production cars are made to be bent and discarded.

In 1951 Porsche for the first time entered a works team in The 24 Hours of Le Mans. Two cars were originally entered. However, both cars were damaged in freak prerace accidents. Out of the remnants, one Le Mans car was glued together. It was a silver-gray light alloy coupe fitted with a tuned 1100-cc engine. Top speed was 100 mph. Two Frenchmen, Veuillet and Mouche, were assigned driving chores. Competition was stiff. All-out racing machines were entered by rival teams. They made loud noises and looked rough and racy. The Porsche was a series-produced coupe with a smooth soft sound and the look of a turtle. If you patted the hood too affectionately, it would dent.

Opposition respected the Porsche name. But entering only one car in a twenty-four-hour race is absurd if you are a serious contender. Not a chance for you guys in the turtle. Besides, Porsche needs more racing experience. This race is for "big boys."

The starting flag was dropped. With a roar the cars slid into the first turn. Hour after hour passed. The "big boys" dropped out one by one. In a remarkable display of durability, the Porsche buzzed on lap after lap. When the checkered flag was displayed, the production Porsche was first in its class. Italian, French and English drivers left the track muttering colorful epithets about that silly German car.

Although the win was only in class, it was a feather in the Porsche hood. The Porsche reputation grew. Orders rolled into the factory after each win. Racing was profitable in knowledge gained and in orders received.

Since Porsche was originally a design firm, ideas and innovations were expected to parade off the drawing boards in never-ending succession. They did. Some of the concepts were dismissed as "too far out" or "not for us." Other ideas were shaped into physical form.

In 1952 the innovation consisted of brakes with a diameter of 280 mm instead of 250 mm. Now the brakes were as "fast" as the car.

A completely synchronized gearbox represented the second innovation. So good was the new gearbox that licenses to produce it were requested by competing firms.

To keep abreast of competition, an all-new car was introduced in 1953. Called the "Spyder," it had an engine with four camshafts, air-cooling blower with a tubular cross-braced chassis and a superlight alloy body, the car really moved! It zipped around the tracks like a spider after a tasty fly—or Ferrari. In the 1954 Mille Miglia Hans Herrmann and Herbert Linge drove it to a first in class. The Spyder's low profile saved their lives during the race when a railroad barrier dropped in front of the car as they were accelerating to 90 mph. There was no time to spin out. They simply ducked their heads and drove under it.

The Spyder also won in class at Le Mans, Rheims and Nurburgring.

Since competition was catching up, Porsche engineers rolled up their design sleeves and produced the Spyder RS and eventually the Spyder RSK.

Engines in these cars were squeezed for more power and speed. Chassis were made lighter for a superior power/weight ratio. Five-speed gearboxes were added for better performance. Bodies were lowered for less wind resistance. Victory trophies and a string of orders again flowed into the factory.

After a brief and unhappy excursion into Formula I racing, in which Porsche shouldered the entire financial burden on behalf of German pride and prestige, the Stuttgart factory entered a new era of racing and racing cars.

Ferdinand Porsche III fashioned an exciting new machine—the 904. This was the start of the series that led to the 917.

Low and lovely, the 904 was a thoroughbred from the tip of her perky, pointed nose to the tilt of her frisky tail. She was a car that would turn the head of a man who was necking with the Playmate of the Year. Even if you didn't race, you needed the 904 for spiritual reasons. You could soothe your soul by looking at her after a hard day at the office.

For the first time Porsche molded a body in fiber glass. Cheap and easy to produce, fiber glass would eventually replace aluminum as *the* material for racing-car bodies.

The plastic body was actually glued to the steel chassis of the 904. Unfortunately, however, the old 4-cylinder engine accompanied this new bullet body, when a completely new engine should have been designed. At its maximum the old power plant developed 195 bhp. Not enough. Too slow.

Although the 904's performance was satisfactory, it was heavier and slower than experts deemed desirable and, beautiful as it was, it failed aerodynamically.

Yet it won its share of races and made Ferrari drivers nervous when it followed the big red cars home in the endurance races.

Soon Porsche developed a new 6-cylinder engine—with chain-driven overhead cams. The racing version of this engine was mounted in a totally new racing car whose existence spelled doom for the beautiful 904.

The new 906 appeared on the tracks at the start of the 1966 season, eager for battle with Ford and Ferrari. The car was a mechanical gem. An ultralight, ultrafine, ultrastrong space frame of steel tubing supported a tough fiber-glass body, providing new measures of superiority. Easy-opening, gull-wing doors allowed fast pit stops. A flat, air-cooled engine was positioned ahead of the rear wheels for greater road stability. Visibility was increased significantly by the addition of the gull-wing doors and an enormous rear window. Rugged and durable, the new cars were extremely fast.

Refinements can be made in any work of art, whether it be a painting or a motor car. Soon Porsche produced the 907, the 908 and the 910.

And they were winners—but only in class, for this was the age of the "big car." Fords were sweeping the circuits and claiming the first prizes.

Ferraris were never far behind the Fords. From time

to time a Porsche would sneak ahead of a Ferrari just to break the monotony.

Then a 3-litre car was brought out by Porsche, and the opponents were in for more surprises. The bigger Porsches started to come in first. These rapid racers won the 1000-km of Nurburgring and the Austrian Grand Prix, causing much alarm in the Ford and Ferrari camps.

Although in 1968 and 1969 a series of races was won in rapid succession by Porsche, the team lost the big race, The 24 Hours of Le Mans. True, in 1969 the Porsche 908 driven by Hans Herrmann lost to a Ford GT by only two car lengths after a twenty-minute nose-to-nose seesaw battle. Still, a loss is a loss. A miss is as good as a kilometer. The international spotlight is on Le Mans. The press is there in battalions. The public is there in swarms. In this, the most visible race on two continents, the winner is bathed in prestige, glory, honors and orders.

The giants of the racing world always won at Le Mans. Porsche was tired of being the manufacturer of cute little cars. The time to be a giant had arrived. The time of the 917 had come.

6 | A Decision to Go Big

The year 1968 was marked by dramatic changes at the Porsche works in Stuttgart.

The primary catalyst for change came from outside the company when the French-influenced Fedération Internationale de l'Automobile (the governing body in auto racing) decreed that in 1968 and extending through 1971 the limit on engine size for sports cars in world-championship long-distance racing would be 5 litres with fifty complete cars presented for homologation. Fifty cars represented a sizable expenditure in a sport where exotic metals are used for common nuts and bolts.

As an option to this rule, the FIA decreed that a team could build as few cars as they chose, providing the engine capacities were restricted to 3 litres. (A 3-litre car will not beat a 5-litre car at Le Mans.)

In any case the big 7-litre American Fords and Chaparrals that seared the tracks the previous year were now outlawed.

When the new regulations were published, a cry of anger went up across the continent and in the British Isles. No one welcomed the new formula. Furthermore, the decree was a complete surprise to all manufacturers. They had spent vast amounts of time and money refining their existing sports cars. Now the labors of the past couple of years would have to be scrapped. To attain a competitive position, either new cars would have to be constructed at great expense or old engines would have to be stretched or reduced. Costly design work was required in any event.

The consensus among those cognizant was: the French-dominated FIA issued the directive to rid the Continent of fast and loud American cars, and to give French cars an edge on competition.

The men who control the FIA won't be satisfied until a French car wins Le Mans *and* the World Championship. They'll continue to play cute little games with the rules to help their cause. Unfortunately, they forget what everyone else knows: Frenchmen aren't battlers, they are lovers. True, they enjoy cars, but for the pleasures of a girl in the back seat, not for the greasy intricacies of the engine. (Perhaps they *are* smarter than the rest of us.)

Even the most elaborate official assistance is of questionable value in auto racing. The major French constructors, Alpine and Matra, were unable to take advantage of these legal maneuverings to gain the championship. Alpine didn't possess the high horsepower needed in the big leagues, and Matra experienced severe development problems, missing a major portion of the season.

Criticisms, complaints and loud grumblings about the new formula continued to increase in number and volume. Pressure was applied. The FIA decided to make a concession by reducing the quantity of new vehicles required for homologation from fifty to twenty-five.

Executives at Porsche took quick note of this change. Hushed conversations were held in the cozy VIP dining room. "Twenty-five cars. Not fifty any longer. The costs for complete participation have come down." More conversations were held in the evenings at private homes. Dreams, wishes and old corporate ambitions were discussed. Vague ideas took solid form.

An official council was called in mid-1968. Since Porsche is an entirely family-owned company, unity and speedy decisions are common characteristics of formal board meetings.

Judgments can be rendered at once. Eccentric stockholders spread over a wide geographic area are not a problem with this firm as they are with most firms of its size. Politics does not play an important role at the Porsche works. There are no outsiders to please. No one to appease. Decisions are formed on the simple premise: if it's good for the company, let's do it. Right now!

A decision was rapidly made to provide the millions of marks necessary to develop a big sports car that would race in the new world-championship formula. A deadline was established. In ten months, twenty-five cars must be on display for official inspection. A demanding regimen. However, to secure maximum benefit from the huge investment, swift design and production work were essential.

This new car, baptized "917," would have 12 cylinders with an initial capacity of 4.5 litres—a giant compared to the biggest Porsche at that time, which measured a modest 8 cylinders for 3 litres.

In 1968, while the new car was being designed,

Porsche lost the Le Mans race once again. A wave of ever-increasing dissent shook the executive suite. The younger members of the family demanded results.

"But we have the 917 under development."

"It won't be ready until next year. And then time will be needed to sort it out. We need action and changes now."

"Perhaps you are right."

"We must win Le Mans, or the world will think we're incapable of such a major accomplishment."

Sensing criticism of his abilities, Porsche racing manager Baron Huschke von Hanstein turned in his stopwatch and retired to his estates. However, he didn't completely sever his relationship with the Stuttgart firm. He continued to serve as a racing and personal public relations consultant to Ferry Porsche.

Von Hanstein boasts a long association with Porsche. Way back in August, 1951, he drove one of the first Porsche automobiles, an 1100-cc model, in the Liège-Rome-Liège Rally—a grueling contest—finishing second in class. Shortly thereafter he was named press officer, and subsequently he directed Porsche's racing efforts. Throughout the early days of his tenure, he continued to race on such circuits as Spa and Targa Florio.

Congenial, intelligent and efficient, von Hanstein was ideally equipped to handle the mercurial temperaments of eager young drivers and the multiplicity of problems attendant to a small manufacturer getting started in international racing.

He was often heard warmly wishing his drivers "good luck." He cared for them as individuals, as people, not only as tools for victory. And this humanity is a rare thing in big-time racing. Yes, von Hanstein was one of the "greats" of racing, as a person and as a professional.

Rico Steinemann, a writer-driver, was quickly hired to take over von Hanstein's positions as team manager and public relations director.

Tall, rangy Steinemann had earned a reputation as an authority on many phases of auto racing. Not only was he a successful driver who placed second at Le Mans in 1968, but he was also a regular member of the Swiss Hartski team. He managed a pit for Jack Brabham, and he gained additional exposure to the racing scene as editor of the highly regarded Swiss magazine *Powerslide*. With his diversified background, Steinemann was judged the man to lead the Porsche cars to a victory at Le Mans.

Youthful, ambitious and a bit autocratic, Steinemann immediately set about reorganizing Porsche racing-team structure. Star drivers were lured away from competing teams in a clever coup. Engineers were prodded to accelerate the development of the 917. His presence was soon felt throughout the Porsche plant. His long-legged strides were familiar in every department.

A Le Mans win was his major goal. He would do all that was necessary to secure it.

7 | Putting It All Together

By the time the first 917 was ready to race, many engineers had worked day and night. Time was at a premium. This car, the most ambitious Porsche project to date, had to be completed and ready for the track ten months after the "go" signal was given by Porsche top management. The normal development time of a specialized racing car is considerably longer than ten months. The slim time period was almost an impossible challenge. Two or three years would have been more realistic.

Hans Mezger, an engineering genius, was put in charge of engine development for the 917. This gentle, soft-spoken man guided the efforts of a brilliant twelve-man team from a small dreary office hooked on to the giant, modern engineering-drafting bullpen at the Porsche works. He found the assignment thrilling, but formidable.

After receiving the news of his new responsibility from management, he returned in a quandary to his crowded desk. "How do I design this enormous engine that absolutely will not fail on the track? What's more, how do I do it in the allotted time?"

He slumped over his desk searching for answers, knowing he could not afford the luxury of error. The small man who usually had a twinkle in his friendly brown eyes scratched his head. Then he lit a cigarette. He was more nervous than usual. He reached into his large desk drawer and pulled out a sheaf of blueprints. Scattering them on his desk, he traced his finger over them. "Yes. Yes. The old 908 engine must serve as the basis for the new powerplant. The expansion will come here. And here. I'll enlarge upon it. Draw it out. The 908 has brought us much success. It is the correct direction."

He pulled out a large pad and began to sketch rapidly. The ideas were pouring out now. He scribbled furiously and long, chain-smoking all the way.

Hans Mezger, chief racing-engine engineer at Porsche, had been employed by the Stuttgart auto firm for thirteen years when he was given responsibility for Porsche's most monumental effort in racing. A graduate of the technical institute in Stuttgart, he had never worked anywhere else. Porsche was home. Developing the 917 was a cherished honor. The challenge pleased him.

A worried young engineer walked into Mezger's small office, sat down and said, "The world will watch our efforts carefully. We mustn't fail. If we do, they will say that Porsche is not capable of producing a big car."

"Don't worry. We'll do it."

"We need time for testing. More time. More time."

"We'll do it."

"How?"

"You just said how. By *testing*. By comprehensive testing." Mezger smiled.

The junior engineer rubbed his chin. "But, Mr. Mezger, is that the complete answer?"

"It's the only answer. We'll utilize our special stress-intensity program to an optimum level. Normal time requirements will be slashed."

"Then preassembly testing will be the key?"

"Right. Through a comprehensive testing program, each piece of metal will be pushed to the absolute limits. We'll know the breaking point of each component before the engine ever gets near a racetrack. It's the only way."

Mezger took time out to light another cigarette. Blowing a cloud of smoke, he continued: "Field conditions will be simulated as we go along. We will be thorough. Complete. Our engine will be ready on schedule, come hell or high water. And it will work. Beyond a shadow of a doubt, the new engine will have the necessary power and endurance to succeed at Le Mans. This is a great opportunity for you, for me and for Porsche. Failure is not conceivable."

Clocks were ignored during the period when the 917 engine was being structured. The project was considered a labor of love by all involved. The old Porsche loyalty was glowing in the hearts of the engineers. Everyone was eager to contribute all he could. Enthusiasm ran high.

The big day finally came. The teapots were washed and the blueprints were filed and the tired eyes were rested and the wives were made happy. The prototype engine was complete. Finished.

The beautiful, complex construction of gleaming metal

parts was placed trophylike on a table previous to final testing.

Mezger plus a few engineers and mechanics gathered around the engine, bathing it in tender glances. After all, it was their baby. And what a baby! Big. Solid. Potent-appearing, with twelve sparkling breather stacks, a network of multicolored wires grouped in an orderly fashion and a large cream-colored plastic air-cooling fan on top.

Subsequent tests indicated that the 4.5 engine produced 520 bhp at 8500 rpm. The power—the necessary punch to win at Le Mans—was there.

Mezger's calculations were correct. Utilizing every scrap of past experience, he designed the 917 to have the same cylinder dimensions as the successful 908 (85-mm bore, 66-mm stroke). The engine was cooled by air. Really cooled. At top rpm the whirling fan drew in 2400 litres of air each second! It was heavy. And it was big. Weighing over 600 pounds, the 12-cylinder power plant measured 30 inches long, 30 inches wide and 26 inches deep. Since it was an opposing engine, the cylinders were set parallel to the ground, with the connecting rods slamming at each other.

The crankshaft featured a unique central drive mechanism that eliminated dangerous vibrations within the engine. Made of case-hardened, chrome-nickel steel, the crankshaft aided in the transmission of power to the gearbox via a central pinion that drove four camshafts, the ignition distributor, the cooling-system blower *and* the alternator.

To keep friction losses down, all Porsche engines feature dry-sump lubrication. The 917 was no exception.

Seven pumps moved the oil around—one pressure

pump and two scavenging pumps in the crankcase, plus four scavenging pumps to insure dry camshaft housings.

For simplicity of construction and weight-saving purposes, there were no oil lines as such. Oil was routed through several of the structural frame tubes that held the 917 together. When the oil in the tubes became excessively hot (over 85 degrees centigrade), a thermostat sent it to a cooler in the nose, chilled it, and sent it out to do its job once again. Nothing was left to chance. The engineers tried to think of everything.

Connecting rods were made of expensive but light titanium, as were the screws. Porsche has had over eight years' background using titanium rods without any unpleasant experiences. So convinced are they of the superior qualities of titanium rods that they would use them in their street or series cars without hesitation—if it weren't for the expense.

Oil throughput was reduced and lubrication improved by the use of collar-end bearings.

The big 917 engine was a mechanical marvel—modern, sleek, trouble-free and tough. All tests put Mezger in the hero's spotlight. He had performed his job well.

Simultaneously with the development of the engine, a chassis, suspension and gearbox for the 917 were being produced. Helmut Flegl, manager of the engineering department—experimental racing section—was in charge of nonengine projects. A young man with determined eyes, Flegl pushed just as hard as Mezger. Idea followed idea. Le Mans fever had spread to everyone. Duties were clearly outlined. The enormous burden of producing the 917 was carried cheerfully by each man working on the new instrument of speed. No one

In 1968 the Fédération Internationale de l'Automobile decided to reduce the quantity of new vehicles required for homologation from fifty to twenty-five (*Porsche*).

A Gulf Porsche 917 slides around the high banks at Daytona. The 917 teams of Gulf/Wyer and Salzburg battled each other as well as the teams of Ferrari, Lola and Matra (*Porsche*).

The Men Who Made the 917 a Winner

Hans Herrmann

Richard Attwood

Vic Elford

Hans Herrmann. The aging German champion hungered for a Le Mans victory. He had missed the winner's laurels at Le Mans by a scant 100 yards the year before. Revenge – that's what he wanted

Richard Attwood. This calm Englishman shared a Porsche 917 with Herrmann at Le Mans. He believed that he knew the secret to victory. And for once he had the opportunity to test his secret

Vic Elford. A hawk-faced man of unbelievable courage, he posted the quickest time at Le Mans in a 917 during the big Porsche push in 1970

Pedro Rodriguez. When he strapped himself into a racing car, he was transformed from a shy, gentle Mexican into a hard-charging lion who would settle for first place – or nothing

Jo Siffert. His driving technique was as precise as a Swiss watch and as fierce as a blast furnace. He really moved along

(Werkfoto Porsche Abdruck Frei)

Pedro Rodriguez

Jo Siffert

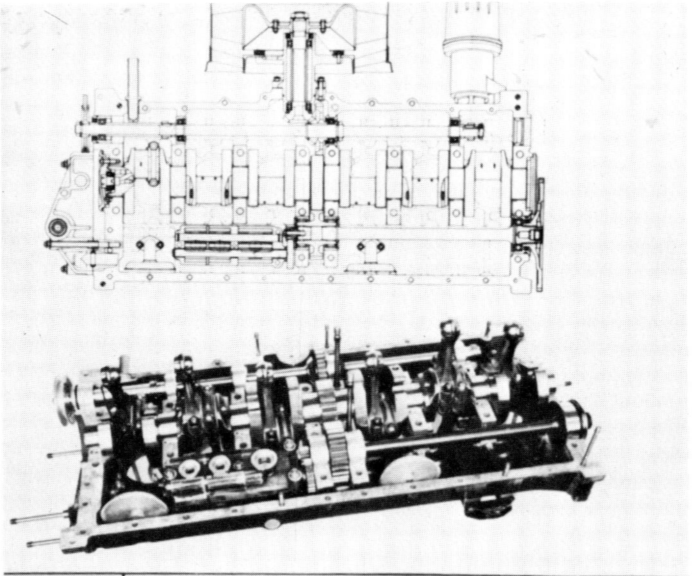

PORSCHE	LONGITUDINAL SECTION RACING ENGINE 917	313.70 ME

(Porsche Audi)

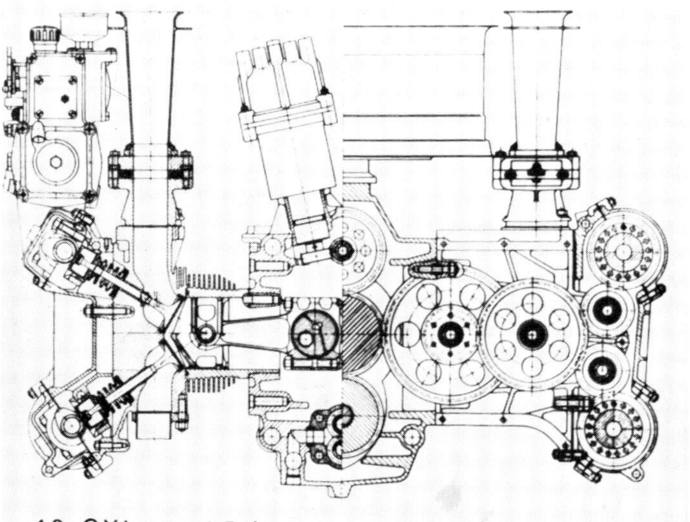

PORSCHE	CROSS SECTION RACING ENGINE 917	312.70 ME

(Porsche Audi)

(Porsche Audi)

(Porsche Audi)

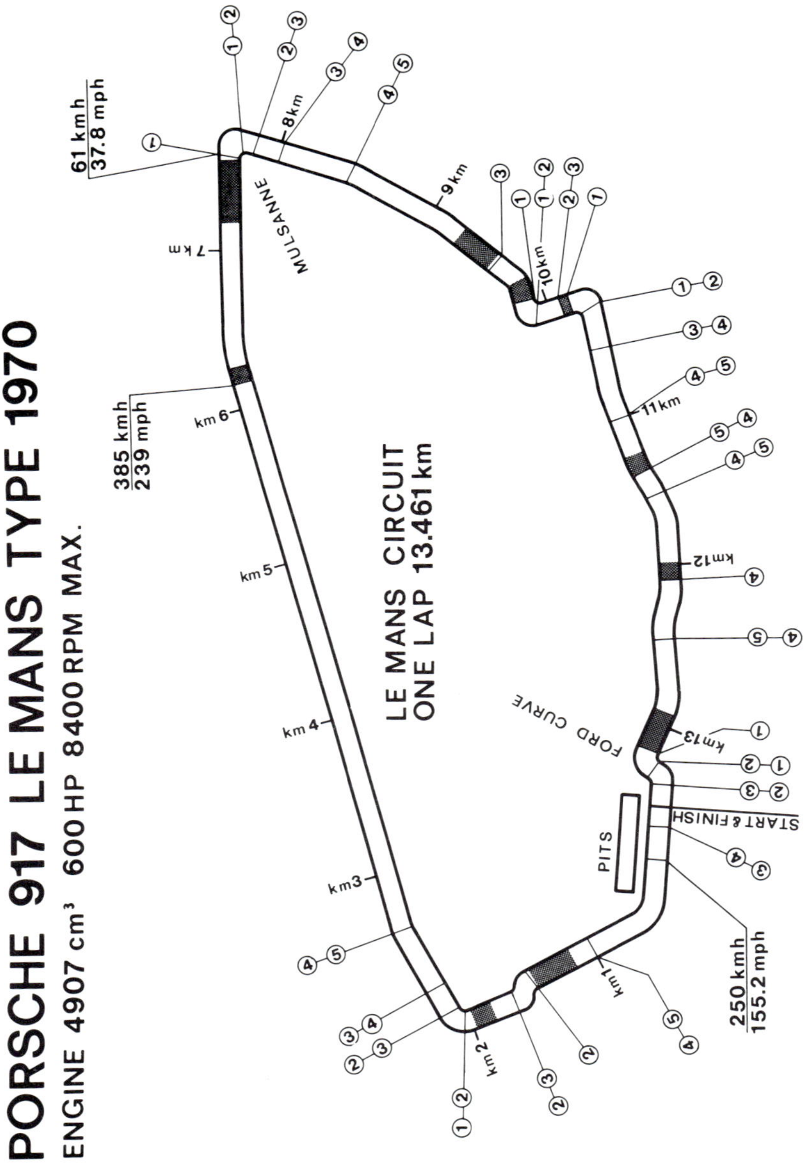

Nothing is left to chance in big-time international racing. This Porsche 917 shift chart for the Le Mans course was computer-produced. Unfortunately the great world of racing is changing from a sport dominated by colorful Red Baron-type drivers to a science controlled by steel-eyed engineers and their bloodless partners – those clicking, clacking, flashing computers (*Porsche*).

Porsche 917 Pre-Race Check List

Event ____________ **Competition No.** ____________

Chassis No. ____________ **Engine No.** ____________

Transmission No. ____________

SECTION A | Engine, Oil and Fuel Systems

Rev: Limiter cutting out at ____________ R.P.M.

Alternator belts inspected for damage
and checked for tension – Front ____________
– Rear ____________

Alternators charging – Front ____________
– Rear ____________

Slow running speed set at ____________ R.P.M.

Exhaust System; Checked for cracks – Primaries ____________
– Tail ____________
– Check manifold bolts locked ____________
– Check primary/tail connection good ____________

Oil System – Oil tank contents ____________
– Grade of oil ____________
– Condition of oil (new, used) ____________
– Oil filter condition ____________
– Oil filter secure ____________
– Check all hoses – for leaks ____________
– for damage ____________
– Check tank for leaks ____________
– Check oil cooler – for leaks ____________
– for secure mounting ____________
– Check all unions lockwired ____________
– Check all hose clips tight ____________
– Check stone guard secure ____________
– Empty catch tank ____________

Fuel System – Check main fuel tanks and collector tank
– for leaks ______
– for mountings ______
– for damage ______
Check all fuel hoses for leaks ______
– for damage ______
– lockwire unions ______
Check fuel pump operating ______
Check fuel pump electrical connections
secure ______
Check fuel pump mountings secure ______
Check fuel filter condition ______
Check ignition coils secure ______
Check plugs & H.T. leads correctly fitted & secured
engine, switch off each distributor in turn
to check operation. ______
Check starter motor secured ______
Check starter motor leads secured ______

SECTION B | *Transmission*

Check transmission casing for cracks ______
Check gear selection: 5th ______ 4th ______
3rd ______ 2nd ______
1st ______ Reverse ______
Examine gear shift linkage ______
Lubricate linkage as necessary ______
Transmission oil condition ______
Double check – Oil level ______
– Grade of oil ______
Transmission oil pipes – Check secure ______
– For lockwire ______
– Check for damage ______
Air ducts – Check mountings ______
– Examine for damage ______

Clutch free play __________

Pedal travel, clutch disengaging __________

Cable condition __________

Cable end connectors __________

Drive Shaft: Examine shaft for cracks __________

Rubber coupling, examine for cracking __________

Universal joint, condition __________

– lubrication __________

Check nuts & bolts secure & loctited __________

Note 1. Stub axle step-down bolts, tighten to 21 m.kg., 151 ft. lbs., secure with Loctite and grease under head.

Note 2. Allen head drive shaft bolt–secure with Loctite, check bolt head does not foul joint. __________

Wheel drive pins, check secure Front _____ Rear _____

Wheels, examine for damage & cracks.

Front _____ Rear _____

Tyres, examine for damage Front _____ Rear _____

Wheel nuts secured Front _____ Rear _____

Engine and transmission mountings secure __________

SECTION C | *Suspension, Brakes, Steering, Frame*

Frame

Pressure test and record leakage

Rate: From _____ p.s.i to _____ p.s.i in _____ minutes

Examine frame in area of suspension mounting points,

– Front upper wishbone, L.H. _____ R.H. _____

– Front lower wishbone, L.H. _____ R.H. _____

– Front spring mounting, L.H. _____ R.H. _____

– Rear top link, L.H. _____ R.H. _____

– Rear lower wishbone, L.H. _____ R.H. _____

– Rear radius arm, upper L.H. _____ R.H. _____

– lower L.H. _____ R.H. _____

– Rear spring mounting L.H. _____ R.H. _____

– Engine and transmission mountings __________

– Detachable tubes, check for cracks ________

– check secured ________

Front Suspension

Check and record wheel bearing clearance,

L.H. ______ R.H. ______

Examine *all* ball joints (for wear & alignment)

L.H ______ R.H. ______

Examine top wishbone L.H. ______ R.H. ______

lower wishbone L.H. ______ R.H. ______

hub carrier L.H. ______ R.H. ______

hub L.H. ______ R.H. ______

Check anti-roll bar free ________

– Secured ________

– No excessive bearing wear ________

– Set correctly (no pre-load on level ground) ________

Check locking pins secure for top and bottom hub ________

Carrier ball joints, L.H. ______ R.H. ______

Check *all* inboard mounting bolts secured ________

Check shock absorbers for damage L.H. ______ R.H. ______

– for leaks L.H. ______ R.H. ______

Steering

Check steering arms for bending ________

– cracking ________

Check track rods for bending ________

– cracking ________

Check toe-in nuts locked ________

Check steering rack free ________

– No excessive play ________

Check steering rack lubricant ________

Check steering universal for wear or damage ________

Examine steering column for overloading ________

Examine steering column mounting bracket for overloading ________

Check steering wheel straight____________

Examine steering wheel spokes for cracking____________

Examine wheel rim for fraying of stitching____________

Check adjustment in correct place____________

Ensure adjustment locked____________

Rear Suspension

Check and record wheel bearing clearance

L.H.______ R.H.______

Examine *all* ball joints (for wear & alignment)

L.H.______ R.H.______

Examine top link,	L.H.______	R.H.______
lower wishbone	L.H.______	R.H.______
upper radius arm	L.H.______	R.H.______
lower radius arm	L.H.______	R.H.______

Check anti-roll bar free____________

– Secured____________

– No excessive bearing play____________

– Set correctly (no pre-load on level ground)____________

Check *all* inboard mounting bolts secured____________

Check locking pins secured in ball joints____________

Brakes

Line pressures set at Front____________ Rear____________

Balance bar set square to pedal when loaded____________

Check for leaks; – Calipers

Left Front____________ Right Front____________

Left Rear____________ Right Rear____________

– Master cylinders

– Bundy piping

– Reservoir

Examine brake hoses for, leaks____________

– Damage____________

– Alignment & possibility of fouling suspension____________

Lockwire caliper bolts, L.F.__________ R.F.__________
L.R.__________ R.R.__________

Check condition of pads, brand new__________
new but bedded__________
Part worn__________

Backing plate edges fitted__________

Quick release clips refitted, L.F._____ R.F._____
L.R._____ R.R._____

Calipers square & central to disc, L.F._____ R.F._____
L.R._____ R.R._____

Brake disc condition, L.F._____ R.F._____
L.R._____ R.R._____

Disc run-out, L.F._____ R.F._____
L.R._____ R.R._____

Pistons free L.F.__________ R.F.__________
L.R.__________ R.R.__________

Reservoirs filled, Front__________
Rear__________

Pedal pumped__________

Brake cooling ducts – Secure__________
– Undamaged__________

SECTION D | Bodywork and Electrical

Check head and pass lamps for operation__________
– for security of fixing__________

Cover headlamp perspexes with polythene
(when required)__________

Check competition number illumination & identification lights (when required)__________

Ensure competition number illumination and rear lamp bulbs can be changed quickly during race if necessary__________

Check tail lights_____ Stop lights__________
Direction flashers__________

Check battery condition ________
Check battery acid fitted ________
Check battery and earth leads secure ________
Check wiper motor operating ________
Examine wiper arm for security and free pivots ________
Examine blades for condition ________
Fill washer bottle ________ Check washers ________
Check panel lights ________
Check spare fuses taped in car ________
Check alternator to regulator cable secure ________
Check regulator fixing secure ________
Check oil warning light operating ________
Check brake pad wear light operating ________
Check tachometer operating ________ Telltale Zeroed. ________
Check oil pressure gauge operating ________
Check oil temperature gauge ________
Check ignition switch secure and operating ________
Check dashboard illumination ________
Check fire extinguisher mounting & test warning light ________
Check front panel secured ________
Examine door hinges for cracking ________
Check door catches secure and operating ________
Examine windscreen for cracks ________
Examine rear view mirror mounting ________
Examine perspexes for damage and fixing ________
Examine rear panel hinges for cracks ________
Examine rear panel fasteners for cracks & check operation ________
Examine spare wheel mounting ________
Check spoilers, equal and in line ________
Check competition numbers ________
Check safety harness undamaged ________
Check tools installed (if required) ________
Check seat fixing secure ________
Screen clean ________

SECTION E | Final Cockpit Check

Check seat in correct position for first driver ______

Check feel of steering ______

Check feel of brake pedal ______

– clutch pedal ______

– accelerator pedal ______

Check mirror set for first driver ______

Check no loose tools, nuts, bolts, etc. on floor or in passenger's seat ______

Check gear shift ______

SECTION F | Race Morning Checks

Oil

Fuel

Dampers

Tyres–race ones fitted

Tyre pressures

During the primary testing period the brakes were less than satisfactory. The end result was internally air-cooled disc brakes of 1.1-inch (28-mm) width screwed to titanium mounting caps, combined with four-piston brake calipers.

Two body designs were molded: the 917L long-tail and the 917K short-tail. As the designations indicate, the 917L had a longer body than the 917K. The 917L enjoyed the advantage of a higher top speed but suffered the disadvantage of instability. Win a point, lose a point.

Everyone admitted the shape of the 917 was not perfect. At times the car seemed determined to leave the ground. Lord knows, it went fast enough to fly. Since few racing drivers own a pilot's license, spoilers were tacked on the front to hold the car on the earth. Later these spoilers were abandoned because overzealous drivers had the unfortunate habit of knocking them off on corner markers, pit walls and other cars.

A movable rear stabilizer that produced a modicum of downward thrust was declared illegal during the 1969 Le Mans prerace inspection, although after a lengthy and serious discussion between race officials and Porsche executives, the cars were allowed to participate with the stabilizers intact and operating.

The original finished car was an uneven blend of shape and form, machinery and motion. It was catlike in appearance and disposition—sleek, graceful and unpredictable, with the nasty habit of biting the hand that drove it.

A large plexiglass windshield provided excellent visibility for the driver, who was placed in an unusually forward spot, with his feet pressing on the car's nose and his back resting on the engine, which was positioned in the center of the vehicle for improved deceleration.

For all practical purposes the entire rear of the car was engine—one big powerful engine.

Weight distribution between the front and rear wheels registered at a 40:60 ratio. Because titanium, magnesium and fiber glass were used in lavish amounts on the 917, its total weight was the same as that of a Volkswagen "beetle."

The 917 project began in earnest in June, 1968. In April, 1969, twenty-five cars were ready to be inspected by members of the FIA. According to the rules set forth by the FIA's Appendix J, Group 5 for long-distance racing from 1969 through 1971, a manufacturer was required to produce twenty-five cars for inspection before one car could be raced in official competition.

Mezger and Flegl had accomplished the seemingly impossible. They had performed admirably under the most severe odds. Attesting to their remarkable achievement is the fact that Porsche personnel developed all major and most minor components. The 917 was not pieced together from various auto-equipment suppliers' parts bins. It was an original work.

The moment of truth was at hand. Completed cars were now available for serious testing. Nearly $1.25 million had been spent shaping this automobile. The gamble was strictly big-time.

Mechanics rolled two 917s into a van that was soon speeding to a nearby testing track.

At the track the 917s were gingerly and lovingly unloaded and pushed through the deserted paddock area to the starting line. "Don't damage them now," someone said "We have only twenty-five in the world."

The driver walked up to the white car and patted it on the hood and smiled. Then he strapped on his helmet. "I'm ready."

One of the engineers opened the curved door. "Go easy at first. Get the feel of it. The top speed on the straight should be favorable. You'll like it."

The driver eased in, clicked on the seat belts and turned the ignition switch. The engine coughed, then caught. He put it into gear. Slowly the 917 moved out. The speed increased. Taking the first turn smoothly, the driver seemed to be in control.

Smiles flashed between the watching and waiting engineers who sensed a job well done. They nodded happily.

Increasing his speed, the driver began to test the car in earnest. With an increase in speed the car twitched and veered in the corners. Spinning the wheel back and forth, the driver was able to maintain control.

As the engineers had predicted, the 917 was fast on the straights. "This could be the car they're looking for," the driver thought. "She moves out well. Like a space rocket. Here's another corner. Oh-oh. There goes the rear, sliding away. Good. Caught her. Easy, sweetheart. Don't be witchy. That's it. That's it, baby."

Approaching a short straight, he worked his way through the five-speed gearbox. Although the straights were sheer heaven, the corners were becoming increasingly hellish as his speed went higher and higher.

Power. The car had that. Beyond question. She could fly away. Nothing wrong there. However, definite problems were becoming apparent as the driver threw the 917 around the track. He couldn't get into the corners as deeply as he wanted because of the loose action of the brakes. Something was wrong with the body shape—or the suspension. She lurched in corners. She had to be worked hard. He was actually perspiring as he corrected and countercorrected.

Deciding to take a corner at a competitive racing speed, the driver downshifted to third and set up the 917 to drift through. The long sleek car refused to be pushed. The tail swung around without warning. Working hard, the driver spun the wheel and downshifted. The car flew from one side of the road to the other, spinning around and around and around like an immense propeller.

First a fence came into view. Then a tree was brushed. Clouds of dust rose as the wheels skidded off the pavement and dug into the dirt apron. A front fender ripped off. Then a tail section and the stabilizer sailed through the air in a giant arc, shattering into a fiber-glass jigsaw puzzle when they hit the ground. The new, costly 917 finally came to a crushing halt against an embankment. The once-beautiful car looked as if it had been butchered by a madman with a dull ax.

Mezger and Flegl ran to the broken car.

"What happened?" they asked the unharmed driver, who was sitting next to the 917.

"She likes to dance into corners. Just won't settle down. Funny girl, this 917."

More engineers ran up. The exhilaration of a job completed on schedule had faded into despair of a project destroyed. An air of tragedy hovered over the scene. No one said anything. A junior engineer half-heartedly kicked a piece of broken fiber glass. Two men looked under the body, taking notes on a clipboard pad. Gloom hung low.

The driver tried to sound optimistic. "Come on, fellows. Successful tests will follow."

Adjustments and modifications were made. And successful tests did follow. But so did unsuccessful tests.

The car was not a perfect machine when the 1969 racing season opened.

Only exceptionally skilled pilots could handle the fire-breathing, jumpy 917. What's more, certain drivers were refusing rides—an unheard-of situation in a profession when men usually bang on doors, begging to drive anything—without pay. Even works drivers with great loyalty to Porsche used unlikely excuses to keep out of the 917's cockpit.

During the first couple of races in 1969, the 917 twitched all over the roads. Its conduct did little to enhance its reputation.

A private driver, John Wolfe, bought the first non-works 917 that was for sale, entering it in the 1969 Le Mans race. His codriver refused to drive it after running a few practice laps. There was an appeal for help, and Herbert Linge, a works driver, was drafted to join Wolfe in the battle of Le Mans. In the end, Linge was not required to put forth great effort. On the very first lap of the race John Wolfe crashed at White House. The car exploded in a great rolling puff of flame and smoke. Wolfe died. The 917 had tasted blood.

Two works cars went on to race at Le Mans in 1969 without great distinction. Both dropped out with clutch troubles, although the last 917 to fail was leading the race when it succumbed.

The big Porsche was not behaving as a dutiful race car should. It seemed to have a mind of its own. Now in addition to instability in the corners, it had taken to wandering down the straights at speed. Engineers and stylists collaborated, scratched heads and produced one corrected drawing after another.

Was the million-dollar thoroughbred just a sick turkey

after all? Having received exhaustive coverage by the world press, the car was becoming a source of acute embarrassment to Porsche. It should have been a winner. The wind tunnel and the computer had said so.

A management decision was reached. A comprehensive team setup was required. Organization. Critical testing. And an outside eye. All this was needed. The 917 was a physical entity now. The myriad details of research and refinement, plus the logistics of running the team, could be better performed by a specialist in this field. Time was short. Competition had seen the 917 at speed. They would attempt to match or better that speed at the earliest possible date. A solid, experienced racing team was needed. Now.

8 | 917 Racing Teams

The average life span of a racing car is two years. At the end of this brief period, the car is totally obsolete. Last year's winner is this year's loser. In motor racing, research and development moves at a highly accelerated tempo. Improvements are hatched at a geometric pace.

A series of irritating problems hampered the rapid development of the 917. The car was unstable at high speeds. The brakes were not as quick as they should have been. There were rim problems and there were tire problems. The long-tail's body flexed, causing jaded drivers to pray. Occasionally the car would leave the ground. Solutions must come. Soon. Time was critical. The 917 would have to be sorted out quickly and thoroughly.

Development engineers never sleep. They live with racing problems. Many of these dedicated men attend every scheduled race. They know that their counterparts on competing teams are doing the same. The pressure is immense. They must produce. They must alter the existing car so it can roar down the straights faster, go deeper into the corners, accelerate with more neck-snapping velocity and remain in almost one piece after absorbing a ferocious beating over extended periods of time.

Then there was the question of a team. A factory simply doesn't decide to go racing and then magically appear at races with cars in top competitive order. A team must be formed to originate strategy for each race, to prepare the cars, to test new components, to eliminate existing bugs, to rebuild semidemolished cars, to select drivers, to arrange for passports, to arrange for customs clearances, to secure entry permits, to provide insurance and driving licenses for the mechanics, to be certain team members have the proper inoculations, to book hotel accommodations for drivers and mechanics, to locate a garage in the vicinity of the track, to insure that drivers, mechanics and cars get to the race on schedule, and to separate drivers' wives and girl friends when they fight. An organization is essential. A separate racing body is needed—a unit divorced from factory activity or an independent subunit located on the premises of the manufacturing firm.

Porsche executives decided to establish a working relationship with J. W. Automotive Engineering, Ltd., of Slough, England, an organization noted for team management and racing-car development. The Wyer people were set up to handle the 917 immediately—at a minimum of expense.

The first feelers were sent out at a cocktail party in Sebring, Florida, in March, 1969.

John Wyer and his racing manager, David Yorke,

were standing in the corner of a crowded, smoke-filled room chatting about the race their team had just won. Neither man enjoyed these parties, but attendance was an obligation, a pit in the cherry pie.

Rico Steinemann, Porsche's public relations man, came over to Wyer and Yorke, flashed his boyish smile and said, "You fellows did extremely well today."

Wyer replied, "Thank you, Rico."

Steinemann twisted out his strong Gauloise cigarette in a nearby ashtray. Casually he asked, "Have any plans for next year?"

Wyer let Yorke do the talking. "Well, you know, Ford is cutting back on its racing program. Bowing out of sportscar racing actually. But we do have a project or two in the works. Can't be left hanging, you know. Always plan ahead."

Steinemann leaned against the wall. He looked down at his drink, rotated it in his palms, watched the swirling amber liquid for a second, then said, "I'd like to suggest a direction for your organization to take during the coming season. You know about our 917. We feel it has great promise. It can be a winner. True, a little more development work is needed." He paused. "That's where you fellows can enter the scene."

Yorke said, "How's that again?"

"We'd like the Wyer organization to be the official Porsche factory team. Help with the development. Run the cars on the circuits of the world."

Wyer stared at him in amazement.

Yorke squinted as if he had a hearing problem. "You want *us* to be your official factory team?"

"That's right. You will be *the* Porsche factory team."

"Well! Well—well. . . ."

Steinemann asked, "What do you think?"

Wyer said, "Naturally we are flattered that the Porsche firm would want us to run their cars. I think that the next step would be to consult our sponsor, Gulf Oil."

"Then, gentlemen, you accept the proposition in essence?"

Wyer and Yorke exchanged glances and Wyer responded, "Yes. Of course."

The three men paused as a conversation-stopping blonde swam by.

After she disappeared in traffic, Rico Steinemann said, "I'm pleased that you accept the plan. Our lawyers must meet soon to arrange the details. Good-bye."

"Good-bye, Rico," Wyer and Yorke said in unison.

After Steinemann left, Yorke said, "Surprised, eh?"

"My, my." Wyer smoothed down his already smooth black hair.

"This solves our problems concerning next season."

"Certainly does. We won't have to produce an entirely new car. One is being handed over to us."

Yorke said, "And if it's a Porsche, it's a good car. No doubt about that."

"Bit unusual, though, for a company of Porsche's size to hand over their racing effort to a small firm like ours."

"John, times have changed."

A few days later John Wyer contacted representatives from Gulf Oil and informed them of the proposal made by Porsche.

At first Gulf's response was less than enthusiastic. They were willing to pay some of the bills when Wyer was running Fords. The benefits were obvious. Ford vehicles were everywhere. Ford sold cars and trucks all over the world. The greatest concentration of Ford vehicles was in the United States. And Gulf sold more of its products in the U.S.A. than in any other country. Sponsoring Ford/Wyer made sound economic sense. But Porsche/Wyer? Porsche was a midget compared with Ford. Furthermore, Porsche was a European company. Gulf didn't have a distribution organization throughout all of Europe. As a result, a portion of the money would be wasted as an advertising expenditure.

The counterargument went like this: If the 917 does indeed win at Le Mans and Monza and Daytona, and if Gulf is very obviously a sponsor, gasoline sales will soar—no matter which car the man on the road is driving. The psychological implication was: If the winning car at Daytona used Gulf gas, your car will be a winner too if *you* use Gulf gas. Gulf gas will turn your Chevy into a 917 Porsche and you into Hans Herrmann.

The contract was signed with Gulf. The 917s would be listed officially as Gulf/Porsche 917s. The importance of the question of financial sponsorship becomes apparent when it is realized that transportation charges alone for cars, men and equipment from London to Daytona can come to $15,000.

John Wyer made a series of trips to the Porsche factory in Stuttgart. Contract details were ironed out. The Wyer entry would be the official works team. Porsche would supply free of charge a minimum of two cars for every race. Spare parts and engines would also be provided free of charge. As the works team, the Wyer organization would be informed of all development work first. All modified components would be handed over to the Wyer team first. And any development work carried on by Wyer would be shared with Porsche racing engineers.

The Porsche-Wyer contract was signed in August, 1969.

Major problems developed with British customs. Bureaucrats issued a decree ordering Wyer to pay import taxes on the 917 Porsche cars, engines, transmissions and assorted parts shipped into England for his team. He didn't have enough pounds sterling to support a racing team *and* to pay taxes on expensive equipment streaming into England.

Lengthy meetings were held with the customs people. A deaf ear was turned to Wyer. More meetings were held. More deafness. Influential persons were contacted. It was only after these persons stated that the Gulf/Wyer/Porsche 917 teams would bring money and jobs to England that the customs people finally saw the problem from Wyer's point of view.

But who are John Wyer and David Yorke? What makes the English Wyer team so outstanding that a German manufacturer would swallow national pride to sign a contract with them?

John Wyer, a seasoned mentor in the field of competitive sports cars, was born in 1909 in Kidderminster, England. Anxious to get into the racing scene, he quit school at eighteen to take a job as an apprentice at the Sunbeam automobile factory. Wyer selected this firm because it was engaged in grand-prix racing and it was British. In rapid order, Wyer advanced from apprentice to designer at Sunbeam. He then took a job at Solex as a sales and service engineer. It was a good job, but he wasn't happy there. It was not racing. A door opened, and he was hired as business manager for the Monaco Racing and Engineering Company, a firm specializing in preparing race cars for young men with more money than talent.

At this time Wyer tested his abilities as a driver behind the wheels of a Ferrari and an HRG. He decided he wasn't good enough, so back he went to the business side of racing.

The rich boys proved difficult to handle. Again Wyer sought new development. In racing, of course.

Moving to Aston Martin in 1950, he accepted a temporary position as manager of the firm's racing program. He held the "temporary" position for thirteen years. Aston Martin's management liked his quiet, low-keyed, efficient manner of getting things done. Wyer climbed the Aston Martin corporate ladder to the rung of Technical Director and Business Manager.

Wyer's team of Aston Martin sports cars enjoyed considerable success. They were victorious at Le Mans and also won the 1959 World Sportscar Championship. Wyer's international reputation was now secure.

When the Ford Motor Company decided to enter sportscar racing—specifically to win at Le Mans—they went to Wyer for guidance. Ford had money. Wyer had experience. An irresistible combination.

Ford established a small factory in Slough, England, where Wyer and Eric Broadley, of Lola fame, mixed ideas. The ideas coagulated. Ford began to win endurance races.

In an effort to streamline their activities, Ford encouraged Wyer to set up an independent firm to campaign Ford GT40s. Wyer had helped Ford. Now Ford wanted to help Wyer. And that is how J. W. Automotive Engineering, Ltd., came into being in 1967.

But bags of money were needed. (In racing it seems that regardless of how much money is *ac*quired, more money is always *re*quired.) At a critical moment Gulf Oil of America galloped out of the west to join the fledgling firm as a sponsor.

The new team was an instant success, winning the world title as well as Le Mans.

The J. W. team's racing manager, David Yorke, is outgoing, lean and sinewy—a hard man with a sentimental streak. A man to whom young drivers come for advice, Yorke is often seen rocking back in his chair, instructing a rookie on the other end of the phone to accept or decline a ride on such-and-such a team.

Yorke possesses a fierce desire to win—at any cost. His drivers are aware of his standards. They know what is required of them. And they accept the situation.

Yorke's credentials are impressive. During the late fifties, he was racing manager of the famous English Vanwall team, gaining invaluable grand-prix experience at an international level.

In a facetious tone he insists, "When I was young I entered racing to make money. Didn't really love racing, you know."

The Wyer factory, covering an area of approximately 10,000 square feet, is a modest building by any standard. Twenty persons are employed, including Wyer, Yorke and John Horsman, the deputy managing director. Three engineers and seven mechanics round out the staff. Occasionally, Wyer will hire special drivers with engineering backgrounds to run his 917s around a practice track and then analyze the behavior of the car in strictly technical terms. The age of greasy-thumb gut knowledge is past. Science has taken over the motor arena.

In addition to maintaining a fleet of 917s, the Wyer organization builds prototype racing cars for other teams, overhauls Formula I engines for a couple of teams and tunes street cars for special customers.

To be sure, the Wyer team has its critics.

In the view of one world champion: "The team is top-heavy. All the drivers think they are number one. There's no discipline, no pecking order. The drivers are badly paired. They're all fierce men underneath."

Another driver thinks that "the Wyer team makes too many last-minute adjustments, and they never seem to have enough parts at a race. Nonetheless, I think they're the best team around. I'd like to drive for them next year."

To bolster Porsche's chances at Le Mans, executives of the Austrian branch of the Porsche firm decided to field a team of 917s. Gerhard Strasser and Rico Steinemann guided this operation. The Salzburg effort was not as tidy as the more experienced, better organized Wyer endeavor. And yet, it was the Salzburg team that carried the Porsche banner to victory at Le Mans. It was the Salzburg team that learned how to sweet-talk the crusty 917 into blazing along for twenty-four rough hours during a rain-swept Saturday and Sunday in France in 1970.

9 | Getting the Bugs Out

The 1969 racing season was a succession of disasters for the Porsche 917. Potential was displayed, but positive results were few. Since big money had been spent developing the giant racing car, Porsche executives were starting to bite their nails, sensing a monumental failure.

What was wrong with the 917? It seemed determined to veer off the road during every outing. Unlike other Porsches, it was unpredictable on the course. The flying projectile was a handful for any driver to manage. Some men were even afraid to touch the car, like hunters shying away from a wounded tiger.

Now that the Wyer team had been hired to guide the fortunes of the 917 during 1970 and to bring a Le Mans victory home to Stuttgart, the Porsche executive office decided that an extraordinary testing session should be conducted immediately. Wyer personnel and Porsche experts were instructed to get together and cure the

917's ills once and for all. Time was wasting. Pride and money were at stake.

In October, 1969, three days of comprehensive tests were scheduled on the Austriaring near Zeltwig, Austria. Paradoxically, the tests began the day after the 917 won its first victory in the final championship event of the season.

Both John Wyer and David Yorke welcomed this opportunity to get a close-up view of the 917. They were convinced that the car was a sleeping giant, a waiting winner. And they were convinced that they could wake it up.

During testing sessions, racetracks are spooky. Zeltweg was no exception. Stands with empty seats stared down at a cluster of men and high-powered 917s. The noisy throngs that normally border the straight, the corners and the esses were conspicuously absent. Also missing were peddlers of soft drinks, snacks, programs, posters, magazines, bumper stickers, and key cases. Tall, silent pine trees were the only spectators. No cheering, no yelling, no enthusiastic girlish screams to break the silence. A tomblike atmosphere enveloped the scene. It all made the work at hand seem that much more serious.

John Wyer and three Porsche engineers walked around a 917. "Extremely attractive car," Wyer said.

"Thank you," responded a young Porsche engineer without zest.

David Yorke asked, "Well, John, shall we have Brian take a whirl at it?"

"Good idea. Where is he?"

"Right here, Mr. Wyer," Brian Redman said, walking up.

"Ready to have a go at it?"

"All set."
Redman eased into the low-slung car and prepared himself for a test ride. The test car was a short-tail 917. It was rated higher than the long-tail model by all the drivers who had hurled the big Porsches around the tracks in 1969.
Redman switched on the ignition. The motor caught. He gunned it twice and roared away. As the 917 buzzed down the straight, its old problem was immediately apparent to Wyer and Yorke: instability. The 917 wavered, wandered and twitched like a hooked trout.
"She's not much better than she was at the beginning of the season," said Wyer.
"Redman is doing a good job, but the trouble is still there." Yorke pulled up his collar as protection against the autumn air. "Blasted wind." He smoothed down his hair. The group watched Redman run a few laps.
Yorke said, "He's coming in."
The big car came to a stop next to Yorke. Redman slid out and lifted off his helmet.
Yorke asked, "What do you think?"
"She's shaky, David. Shaky."
"Any ideas on solving the problem?"
"Had a thought or two about suspension changes." The two men walked to the rear of the 917.
Yorke stopped suddenly. "Say, look here! I hadn't noticed this before."
Redman looked around, not seeing anything of import. "Where?"
"Here. On the tail."
"I still don't see anything."
"That's it! There aren't any bugs!"
"Bugs?"
"Insects. There aren't any splattered insects on the

tail of the 917. That means the tail isn't receiving an adequate blast of descending air. The aerodynamics are all wrong! That's why the car jumps all over the track. There simply isn't enough downward air pressure on the tail. If there were, the tail would be spotted with dead bugs! The air is moving over the tail, but it isn't applying any downward thrust to speak of. So the tail doesn't obey the driver. It does as it pleases. Downward air pressure is necessary for stability."

Yorke swung around, pointing at two mechanics who were standing nearby. "You men. Bring a few sheets of aluminum, some tin snips and a stapling gun. Hurry. We're going to fix this car!"

Yorke bent over the 917, his gray eyes lighting up. Tracing a shape in the air, he said, "I think the tail should flare up like this. A shape of this sort simply must catch the air. The flow will be thus, exerting a sizable push towards the earth—which is exactly where we want the 917 to remain."

The mechanics returned with their material.

Yorke sketched on the aluminum sheets. "Snip that out."

Engineers gathered around the fabricating unit. Excitement was in the air. The men were murmuring, asking each other hushed questions. What was he doing? Would it work? What's this about bugs? Did he really say "bugs?" Of course not. Yes, he did. I heard it. They stared at John Wyer and David Yorke—legendary heroes of the sportscar panorama. Were they really going to save the 917?

The junior engineers had read about these celebrated men in auto journals and in the sports pages of their newspapers. Now here they were, performing automotive surgery.

The junior engineers had been surprised when the association between Porsche and the Wyer organization was first announced. In the past, Porsche had assumed a highly individualistic posture. The company worked alone. They did things *their* way. Because Porsche had pioneered rear-engined cars and air-cooled engines, the automotive world laughingly asked, "Why don't they build cars the way everyone else does?" But Porsche executives were true to old Dr. Porsche's unique concepts. Their cars won races—and established a sound sales record. Successes prompted one more variation of an old maxim: There's a right way to build cars, a wrong way to build cars and a Porsche way to build cars. Now Porsche was collaborating with a foreign firm—an English firm to boot.

John Wyer took a puff on a thin cigar. In his quiet manner he asked, "Think you have it, David?"

"I'm very optimistic, John."

One of the mechanics held up a flap of aluminum. "All finished, sir."

Yorke reached down. "I'll take it." He marched over to the 917K. "It should be positioned here." The beautiful, sleek appearance of the 917 was being altered radically. "Put another piece here on top. The fender should rise in the rear. The height of the tail at the extreme rear must equal the height of the cockpit. Except for the area immediately behind the engine, the tail section must rise and be enclosed. We want the air to slam down on it."

With stapling guns, the mechanics were fastening the rough pieces of aluminum where Yorke directed.

"Now let's build a little rising flap in the center, behind the engine, connecting the double boxes of the tail."

When the work was completed, Yorke stood back to

inspect the job. "Not very pretty. I'm afraid we've spoiled her beauty. She does look tougher, though."

He looked around. "Brian, would you please take her around the track?"

"Right." Redman quickly donned his helmet and once again slid into the low car. The 917 moved down the straight.

Yorke said, "We'll soon see if that effort was worthwhile."

In short order Redman worked up to speed. Eagerly and anxiously Wyer, Yorke, the engineers and the mechanics lined the track edge to watch the performance. The change in the car was obvious from the moment it entered the first turn. Around and around the track it flew. Drifting here. Controlled sliding there. Always obedient to the driver's command. Never getting overly sassy. Faithful, but certainly not docile. An excellent racing car.

A mechanic exclaimed, "You've done it, Mr. Yorke!" Other enthusiastic voices rang in, "Congratulations!" "Good work!" "She's a sure winner, now!"

Redman pulled up and jumped out. "How were the times?"

"Excellent," said Yorke. "How does she handle?"

"Day-and-night difference. Clings to the road now. The power and the handling are almost in perfect balance. She's not as smooth as silk, but she's not that type of car anyway. She'll always be bold and brassy. She's big and she snorts and she'll bite your finger if you aren't careful. But that's an improvement—she used to go after your whole arm."

During the three days of testing, additional changes were made. Although everyone agreed that the suspension was not the chief villain, the consensus was that it could be improved. Adjustments to prevent anti-dive tendencies were made. Springs and dampers were changed. Camber was altered. All in all, five front-end suspension setups were tried and three rear-end suspension adjustments made before Yorke and his men were satisfied.

They also improved the brake system.

Every inch of the 917 was examined by the testers at Zeltweg. Charts were compiled, checked and double-checked. The car's handling characteristics were carefully scrutinized. The manner in which it entered a corner was recorded. The manner in which it left a corner was recorded. The manner in which it behaved on the straights was recorded. Notations were made of tire wear, brake fatigue, suspension stress and driver strain.

As a result, additional conversions were made for toe-in and roll bars.

Before terminating the tests, David Yorke called the drivers together at trackside. "I'd like to see what she can do now that we've given her a spoonful of medicine and a new shirt. She's in peak condition. She ought to be able to snip seconds off old lap times, cling in the corners, blaze down the straights—and do it gracefully. She should cuddle and squeeze you guys in the cockpit, instead of bouncing, throwing, jolting and generally abusing you. Everything about this car should be easier now: steering, shifting and braking. We've done extensive work on her. She's different from the car we arrived with. She even looks different. Your hands won't get numb. Your shoulders won't ache. Your bodies won't feel as if you had been rolled down a mountainside. She's a good girl. She's going to be one of the most popular cars on the circuits. Because her handling has improved and because she's going to win races, chaps will be waiting in line to drive her—instead of running away from her. She'll be known as a 'classic.' Praised for years to come. She's a great car."

He looked at the drivers, one by one—Brian Redman, Leo Kinnunen and the Porsche works driver, Kurt Ahrens. They appeared more relaxed than they had been three days before. Problems had been solved. The pressure was off. The 917 had been cured of its suicidal tendencies. She was almost a pleasure to drive now. Although still not altogether predictable, she was no longer a savage. Some measure of relaxation in the cockpit was possible. Not every lap was a nightmare.

York slapped the top of the 917. "Let's take her around one more time. See what she can do now that she has been sorted out."

Without saying a word, Kurt Ahrens eased on his helmet and got into the car.

The engine came to life. He watched the tachometer move upward, hit the accelerator and zoomed away, increasing his speed as he flew down the straight.

Setting the car up for the first corner, he depressed the clutch pedal, hit the brake, hit the accelerator, threw the gearshift into third, let out the clutch and slammed the accelerator to the floor.

The 917 took the corner smoothly. None of the old twitching. Ahrens clicked the gearshift lever through the slots to fifth gear. She was moving now. The engine actually screamed in mild protest as Ahrens pushed it to its limits.

Another corner coming up. Brake. Downshift. Drift through. Cinders clattered against the right rear fender as the wheel left the track.

Still demonstrating an independent spirit, the 917

would allow herself to be pushed just so far and then she would object.

Ahrens began his second lap. He was just warming up.

Yorke watched him blaze down the straight. "He's moving. We'll have some good times today." He glanced at his stopwatch. "We certainly will."

With iron nerves and split-second reflexes, Ahrens pushed the 917 further, bent on discovering exactly how good the car was at this point in her short life.

The 917 didn't appreciate this challenge. Going through turn three, she snapped her tail like a London lass attracting a male tourist. Ahrens skillfully spun the wheel, back and forth, arm over arm, in an effort to keep the petulant car from rushing headlong into an embankment.

He steadied the tail and jammed his foot on the gas pedal. Then he threw her in fourth gear. The fat tires stuck to the pavement as he roared on.

"Good girl. Be smooth. Smooth."

Swiftly another corner appeared. Now the 917 raced through in a sweeping slide, obeying Ahrens's every command. He completed the lap without further incident. The car was indeed more docile, more receptive to the delicate manual suggestions of the driver. She was almost graceful, outstanding in the way she handled.

To establish a better lap-time comparison, he circled the course once more. The 917 jiggled a bit in one or two corners, but she did not seriously misbehave.

When Ahrens coasted to a stop, the entire testing crew ran over to him.

"Congratulations. Your time was great."

They slapped him on the back.

Yorke smiled. "Kurt, I think you've proved once and

for all that we have a competitive car here. Look at these lap times."

Yorke handed his clipboard to Ahrens and pointed to the figures.

They spoke for themselves. On the first day of tests the 917 with the original body design had lapped the course at 48.4. Subsequently, as a result of the insect-inspired new body shape, the 917 had sliced the time to 44.2, which represented a significant increase in speed. But now Ahrens had lapped the course at a *still* faster pace. His best new time was 43.3!

Only one question remained to be answered. Could the 917 take it for twenty-four hours? Le Mans would tell.

10 | The Men for the Machines

John Wyer and David Yorke had short-circuited Porsche's computers and wind tunnels as well as the university consultants who had insisted that the 917's body shape was perfectly attuned to racing conditions. Old-fashioned racing experience and a pair of tin snips saved the 917 from a cloudy career as an also-ran. The two Porsche racing teams—J. W. Automotive and Porsche-Salzburg—were now busy making preparations for the 1970 season and the 1970 Le Mans race in particular.

To reach the victor's stand, the teams knew they had to secure the proper driver/car combinations. Although the 917 had been tamed, she was extremely spirited. Not all drivers could steer her accurately around a course.

As David Yorke said, "There are very few good sportscar drivers in the world today. A good sportscar man is relaxed in the heavy traffic that is common to Le Mans. Pressure must not disturb his efforts. This may surprise some people, but I believe a good sportscar driver is harder to find than a good Formula I pilot. Call it heresy, but I believe it."

The Porsche-Salzburg team quickly signed up Richard Attwood and Hans Herrmann as their key pilots. Both were top-rated professionals, and the fact that Herrmann was German was all the more gratifying to Porsche, which is, after all, a German company. What a victory that would be if Le Mans were won by a resident of the Black Forest!

The stars of the Wyer team were Jo Siffert and Pedro Rodriguez. Supporting them, and almost as talented, were Brian Redman and Leo Kinnunen. For the Le Mans race, Wyer entered a third 917 for Mike Hailwood and David Hobbs.

The racing philosophies of the two Porsche teams differed radically, as did their drivers' approach to racing.

David Yorke, racing director of the Wyer team, prefers to hire tough, aggressive men—young chargers who are always motoring on the edge of disaster. Yorke himself is tough and hard-driving. Consequently, he demands those qualities of his drivers. Play-it-safe people will never sit in one of his cars. His men race flat-out from start to finish. The finish could be a checkered flag, an overworked gearbox or an embankment. Naturally, the drivers aren't given instructions to blaze around the track at top rpm, but the competitive personalities of the drivers insure a brisk rate of speed. Wyer Porsches snag either first place or no place. A Wyer car that places second or third is a rare sight.

The Porsche-Salzburg team was conservative by

contrast. The drivers were not flamboyant on the track or in their life styles. Manager Gerhard Strasser was efficient, effective and resourceful in guiding the destiny of his improvised team. Operating under handicaps not experienced by the Wyer team, he did a superb job. For example, he didn't have the autonomy that Wyer enjoyed. He was always under the watchful eye—if not the heavy thumb—of the Porsche factory. Since the Salzburg-Stuttgart relationship was a Siamese-twin situation, he was always obliged to listen carefully. In addition, his facilities weren't as tidy and complete as Wyer's.

Reflecting the Porsche firm's conservative outlook were the driving styles of Attwood and Herrmann. Intelligent and unemotional in their approaches to a race, these men planned a course of action before the event. And, remarkably enough, they stuck to it.

What are these drivers of the lightweight superbomb really like? Let's consider them separately. First Hans Herrmann:

Success followed success for Herrmann in 1953, his first full year in racing. After winning the GT class in the Eifel race, he was asked if he would like to drive at Le Mans. Quite an opportunity, coming during his first full year in racing! Normally a driver has to wait years—constantly polishing his skills—before he is given the chance to race at Le Mans. Herrmann's quick reply was a calm, "Of course." He wasn't calm inside, however.

He did not disappoint the men who believed in him. He drove a streamlined coupe to a class win in the twenty-four-hour contest—an outstanding accomplishment for his first go at the Sarthe circuit.

He didn't let up. After spectacular runs at Schauinsland and the Nurburgring in a Porsche Spyder, he was declared German Sports Car Champion. His star was rising rapidly and burning brightly.

Herrmann and Porsche formed an association early in Herrmann's racing career. In 1954, the Stuttgart firm placed their latest and most valuable machinery in his hands. As a matter of fact, he drove the first 1500-cc, four-cam Spyder in the 1954 Mille Miglia, placing sixth overall and first in class. He finished the year by once again snagging the German Sports Car title for himself and Porsche.

Almost every driver—no matter how careful—has one nasty accident during his career. The accident may occur very early in a driver's career and destroy his nerve, forcing him to take a job driving a milk truck instead of a racing car.

If a man crashes catastrophically in mid-career, he frequently becomes a much more cautious—and slower—driver than he formerly was. Racing writers describe his new driving style as "mature." Actually he has a mature fear in his heart—which is understandable. After nearly being cooked to a crust in a flaming wreck or ground into oatmeal, he has an inalienable right to tremble.

When a driver has an accident late in his career, it usually signals the end of his racing life. He just hangs up his helmet. At this point in time, if he is bright and has saved his starting money, he opens an autoboutique or manufactures racing cars of his own design. The unfortunate ex-driver pumps gas or sells used cars.

Many drivers have the sign of death on them from the very moment they sit in a racing car. Everyone in the business expects them to die—young. They crash. And again. And once more. Then it's over. They were marked. The look was in their eyes. Wild. Intense. Haunted.

Some drivers roar around the tracks at a successful speed, capturing victory after victory without even denting a fender. Their luck is outstanding. Their brakes hold. They never lose a wheel. No one spins in front of them. They race on and on without suffering the slightest injury. Not even a torn fingernail. Then one day it happens. The accident. And the driver will never have another. He is dead. His bowl of luck is broken. And so is he. The men in this category seem untouchable for a while. They seem to be able to drive through flaming chaos unharmed. But racing is like war. If you are a participant long enough, you die. These "one accident" types are usually of world-championship status. The late Jim Clark was a member of this group.

Herrmann had *his* accident while practicing for the 1955 Monte Carlo race. It sent him to the hospital and forced him to take a year's vacation. Every minute of the year was emotional agony. He longed for the touch of the steering wheel.

During 1957–58 he drove for Borgward. In 1959 he was back with Porsche. He understood the little air-cooled cars and they understood him. Furthermore, he had an excellent rapport with the calm Porsche executives.

His luck changed for the better in 1960. Winning the Targa Florio and The 12 Hours of Sebring, he was acclaimed as the best Porsche pilot of the year.

In 1969 he almost captured The 24 Hours, but a

sputtering engine caused him to lose by less than a hundred yards to the Ferrari of Jacky Ickx. His was the only Porsche running at the end.

Car owners and Porsche factory representatives liked Herrmann's unruffled style of racing. He squeezed the most out of a car, but he didn't destroy it in the attempt. Germans don't appreciate crash-and-burn drivers. Racing cars are too expensive to be driven into trees or steel barricades.

Richard Attwood, the other member of the Salzburg team, began to make his mark on the international scene in 1969 when Porsche enrolled him to pilot a 908 Spyder in the Manufacturers' Championship series.

In that year he placed second at Brands Hatch, second at Watkins Glen and fourth at Nurburgring.

Attwood first lowered himself into a 917 at Le Mans in 1969 for practice. He was somewhat reluctant to trust his fragile body to the snorting racer, having heard an alarming number of reports of its unpredictable character. As a result, he toured the course in a cautious fashion, to the consternation of Porsche officials. Attwood says, "I'm the nonheroic type." Nonetheless, he led the contest for several laps until his gearbox broke.

Attwood first scored with the 917 in the 1969 Grand Prix of Austria, where he finished third with codriver Brian Redman. In 1970 he grabbed second spot at the Nurburgring in a Porsche 908 with Hans Herrmann and third at Brands Hatch in a 917, once again with Herrmann as codriver.

Although underrated by some experts, Attwood is a pleasure to watch on the track. Competent. Skillful. Professional. Intelligent. Without breaking a car, he will force it to deliver its ultimate.

The key men on the Wyer team, Siffert and Rodriguez, were fire and rage on the track in contrast to Herrmann and Attwood, who were ice and tranquillity.

Jo Siffert, the oldest member of the team, was born in Fribourg, Switzerland, on July 7, 1936. Articulate, with a multilingual facility, he was at home anywhere in the world. His quiet personal manner was the complete antithesis of his racing style. A charger, Siffert believed that a racing car should be raced. He tried to edge into first place on the first lap and remain there until the last lap. Many times his cars weren't as strong as he. When they were, he won the race.

Siffert roared to the top of the mountain the hard way. There was no money to open doors. No friends in influential places to pass along a good word. He was born of poor peasant parents.

Determined to race, he saved his pennies and bought a 125-cc Gilera motorcycle in 1957. Often he and his mechanic were completely without funds—and without food. With an empty stomach applying pressure, Siffert was forced to develop his skills as a driver. It was win or get thin. In 1959 he decided that regular meals were a worthy ambition, pushed hard and became motorcycle champion of Switzerland.

Switching over to four-wheel vehicles, he continued his winning streak, earning a reputation as one of the fastest men in motor racing.

With great success, he raced in the Formula Junior and Formula I series. However, he was truly outstanding as a sportscar pilot. In 1969 his record was phenomenal. Driving a Porsche 908, he and his codriver captured first place at Brands Hatch, Monza, Spa, Nurburgring and Watkins Glen. He blazed home ahead of the crowd in a 917 at Zeltweg, presenting Porsche with victory number one for the new car at a point in time when the Stuttgart firm's executives were in a state of despair over the car's behavior and future.

In 1970, driving a 917, he snagged first at Spa and Zeltweg. He won Monza in a 908.

A sharp businessman, the moustached Swiss ran a combination autoboutique and Gulf service station in his native Fribourg.

The quest for speed extended into every phase of his life, as demonstrated by his hobbies: skiing, ice hockey and bobsledding. When he moved, he moved fast.

Siffert was a likable fellow who enjoyed a reputation for being loyal to friends and employers. At one point in his career he refused to switch teams to get a better ride because of loyalty to the team manager—a close friend. Friends were special to Siffert. He never criticized any aspect of the 917 or any phase of the Porsche racing program. When reporters asked his opinion of the 917, he inevitably said, "She's a good car."

Jo Siffert died on October 24, 1971, in the flaming wreckage of a BRM Formula I car. His death was unexpected, yet expected—which is true of the deaths of all racing drivers. Siffert didn't fail in a tense moment. His car did. At 160 mph. In an earth bank.

Siffert made many friends during his travels around the world. Many of them paid him a final tribute by lining the road as the cortège moved towards the cathedral of Fribourg. One of his mechanics, Jean-Pierre Oberson, carried Siffert's helmet. His 917 followed, pushed in silence. Many tears were shed that day for this knight of the tracks. He was thirty-five years old.

Pedro Rodriguez was the other star of the Wyer team during the season of Porsche's great assault on Le Mans. Pedro is dead, also. He died in 1971 in a minor race in Germany, piloting a friend's car. A tire blew, throwing him into a wall. The car burst into flames upon impact. Rodriguez died of a fractured skull and severe burns.

Outstanding in both Formula I and sports cars, Rodriguez entered the racing world on a 125-cc Adler motorcycle in his native Mexico at the tender-cheeked age of twelve! The prodigy's career shot ahead like a space rocket. At the age of fifteen he was campaigning a 1500 Porsche Spyder. At eighteen he was racing at Le Mans, and at twenty-eight he won Le Mans driving a GT 40 Gulf-Ford! In 1970, he and his codriver drove the Porsche 917 to victory at Daytona, Brands Hatch, Monza and Watkins Glen.

Another man with a fiery driving technique and a quiet personality, Rodriguez was always pleasant company. He was not a complainer. He accepted life in general, and bad tracks and bad racing weather in particular. As a matter of fact, he delighted in leaving the glamour-stars of racing behind as he rushed around challenging courses during rainstorms.

Fast drivers often become impatient with slower drivers in front of them, especially if they refuse to allow the faster driver to pass. Pedro had a reputation for bumping the slower cars out of the way. Slower drivers found this a bit annoying and somewhat nerve-racking. Often, they would finish the race muttering to themselves.

Pedro was a racing driver. He wanted to be out front at all times under all circumstances.

During a certain race the blazing sun scorched the drivers' eyes, blinding them when they zoomed over a modest hill. Consequently, all of the drivers slowed down as they approached the hill—with the exception of

Rodriguez, who increased his speed, passing competitors along the route. After the race was over, one of his rivals walked over to Rodriguez and said, "Pedro, what was your secret? Why didn't the sun bother you? Tell me your trick."

Pedro answered, "I just closed my eyes when I reached the hill. Then the sun didn't bother me."

Rodriguez was one of the most sought-after drivers at the time of his death. He could take any car and put it at the head of the pack and keep it there until it won or it broke.

A true cosmopolite, Rodriguez was born in Mexico of wealthy parents in 1940, had an apartment in Paris, drove a German car and wore an English deerstalker hat with his racing overalls at the track.

His absence makes the racing circus less colorful, less gay.

These were the key drivers in Porsche's push to victory at Le Mans. These were the men who would risk their lives throwing a 230-mph projectile around a racecourse dotted with a splendid array of death-dealing obstacles, such as trees, steel barriers, earth banks, cement walls and spinning cars.

Why do they do it? What *makes* a driver do it? Is it money? For some, yes. However, those who race strictly for money never reach the first ranks. It is possible for a driver to earn big money in racing. A pro racing for a factory team should average $20,000 a year. And earnings of over $100,000 a year are not uncommon. But not everybody in racing earns a pile. Richie Ginther at age twenty-nine signed on with Ferrari for $160 a month. Dan Gurney also started with Ferrari for the same figure. Racing has men standing at both ends of the financial ladder—with the larger group at the bottom.

Some men pay to race. They buy their own cars, pay their own expenses—which are considerable—and hope to grab some prize money. (Unlikely for an independent.) They hang on, hoping that a factory team manager will notice them. Usually they are first noticed when they crash and die.

During the early days of his career, Pedro Rodriguez's father supported him in racing to the tune of $80,000 a year. Racing cars are expensive.

A few years ago several noblemen were painted into the racing picture. Marquis de Portago, Count Von Trips and Count de Beaufort ran with the leaders. Although money wasn't a problem for these men and their influence was considerable, they, too, had to prove themselves, because when you are out on the track you can't hide. Everyone sees you. You are more than naked. Talent or lack of it becomes apparent rather quickly.

These noblemen were blessed with ability and flair, lending dignity and grace to the profession. Drivers from the lower strata of life imitated their habits, dress and customs. The style that the noblemen brought still permeates the racing circle.

Those noblemen who made it to the first ranks of racing are now dead. Men who have risen from humble beginnings are now in the forefront. The background is dotted with the sons of wealthy businessmen.

The popular image of the American oval-track-racing driver (brash, loud, personally aggressive) does not apply to sportscar drivers. Almost to a man, sportscar pilots are soft-spoken. Although they are internationally famous, they are shy with strangers. Most of them speak two languages. Many speak three. A knowledge of more than one language is a necessity of the trade. During the past season a better-than-average driver was fired from a major team because he wouldn't learn to speak the team manager's language.

All racing drivers are brave. The degree of bravery reaches unimaginable heights. Consider: A man is racing down a straight at 230 mph in a superlight plastic or aluminum car; something snaps; he hits a wall at full speed. Every driver knows this could happen on any ride. He sees it happen to his friends. Yet he races week after week, riding on the thin edge of disaster. Nerve. It takes cold nerve. And concentration. For six hours, twelve hours, twenty-four hours, he must hold the same line through a 100-mph corner or lose a second. Or worse, lose the car. At higher speeds he can't afford to blink.

He has to be fit, trim. Most drivers smoke and drink very little. Many work out. Stirling Moss resembled a middleweight champion. Top physical condition is imperative in endurance races that continue through the day and the night. Vibrations shake the driver's arms. In-car temperatures of over 100° F blister his body. Headlights and exhaustion burn his eyes. Engine fumes sear his throat. The driver must be able to cope with unpleasant physical realities, able to rise above them.

Racing drivers enjoy life. These men who worship at the altar of speed are alive every minute of their existence. They feel life's rush and flow. Their nerve ends are raw from the knowledge that the next time on the track may be the last. Being intelligent, sensitive and observant, they are acutely aware of their universe. Fine wines, fine foods and, in many cases, fine women earn their admiration. They also appreciate music, books and paintings. Oh, a few drivers are one-faceted and sink in a mire of axle grease, bolts and suspension settings, but these are in the minority. Drivers by and large are well-read, widely traveled persons exuding an easy *joie de vivre.*

They are keen to understand and appreciate the richness and depth of life, unlike the average citizen who is awash in a lukewarm world. To a driver, life is a transitory condition. Death is his constant companion. Today is all there is.

Yet they gladly accept their chosen field: their destiny with a guardrail, their brief flash of fury. As one driver said, "I'd rather be a lion for one day than a sheep for one hundred years."

Yes, death is on the track during every event, even the most insignificant club race. She hovers over the circuits like a hungry demon waiting for food. And she gets fed frequently. Some racing teams feed the demon more often than others. And yet there is never a shortage of drivers—for any team.

Most drivers laugh at death. "I'll squeeze her tail before she gets me." They have a contempt for her.

Some are philosophical. "Why worry? She will get you in the end no matter what you do."

A few change the subject or get angry when death is mentioned.

Whatever their attitudes, death is always near them. You can almost smell her. Every time a man sits in a race car, he is issuing a direct and specific challenge to this lady-demon whose hunger is never satisfied. She wants another and another and another. And sooner or later she will get every one of them if they race long enough. And they know it. And they continue to race.

When a reporter recently questioned a driver's disdain for death, the driver asked, "Do *you* expect to live forever?"

Death is waiting at the end of every man's life. Most persons try to hide from this fact. They accumulate dollars, cars, bigger and bigger houses, clothes, color television sets and job titles as if they were going to exist for eternity. They are mean, miserable and petty in their quest for possessions. They'll kick those who work for them and stab those for whom they work. And they die of a heart attack at age forty-six. Or perhaps they *do* reach old age.

The racing driver rejects this conventional mode of life as unfortunate. He would rather accept the presence of death and live three thousand years in every second by doing exactly what he wants to do—and by enjoying it.

Drivers are noted for their hijinks, for their sense of the absurd. And any member of the racing fraternity is a likely victim of hijinks at any time.

Several drivers gather around a table. Diagrams are made. Watches are synchronized. Lookouts are posted. Then everyone runs to the fun. They squeeze a small car into a driver's second-floor hotel room during his absence . . . steal the clothes from a driver and his girl while the couple are in the shower together . . . fill water glasses with straight gin at a victory banquet. And on and on and on. Life to the drivers is a Charlie Chaplin comedy. Funny but filled with pathos.

Drivers don't think about tomorrow or the possible consequences of today's activities. If they did, they would stop racing. Cars break during every race. Many men die at the wheel every year. Don't think about it. Don't think about it.

A noted driver who recently suffered a serious accident apparently does think about it and screams at track owners to effect greater and greater safety measures. Some day he will request upholstered guardrails. At that time the sport will be destroyed. If the risk is gone—if anyone can do it with impunity, why bother to watch?

Still another driver carries a pillbox. On this pillbox is engraved "Everything is sweetened by risk." Perhaps this is the motto by which the average driver lives.

Some drivers are religious. Most are not. Pedro Rodriguez was very devout. He prayed before every race. It didn't save him.

Most drivers are fatalists. "What will be, will be," they say. Pedro said that, too.

Driving is an uncontrollable love affair which the men cannot dissolve. The driver blends his being with the car. The two, car and man, are a single unit in time and space. Through a heightened sensitivity, the driver instinctively knows how to handle, how to respond to his metal bride. Like women everywhere, sometimes she rewards him, often she destroys him.

Drivers frequently discuss the fact that in a potentially fatal accident situation, when the car is spinning and spinning and heading towards a solid barrier, time slows to the point that existence and reality appear to be projected in slow motion. The barrier is there. The car is rushing towards it at 120 mph. But it takes forever to reach it. During the interim, the world is seen in microcosmic clarity. The pebbles on the road are visible. The rough cement surface of the barrier is in crisp focus. A Ferrari is approaching. The driver's eyes are blue. A man selling peanuts at trackside is wearing a soiled white coat. The grass is twelve inches high around the barrier. The barrier is now only six inches away from the car.

Driving at high speed is obviously both an emotional and a physical sensation—a combined sensual and psychedelic experience. As the driver roars along the road, the cars, the grass, the trees, the spectators, the colorful banners swirl and swim and rush through his consciousness in a kaleiodoscopic ethereality. He is floating, rushing, charging, skidding, sliding, missing, passing and winning. Fright mingles with ecstasy. In short, driving at high speed is a totally unreal experience.

In winning, he is the glorious conqueror. Supreme. A knight who, with his faithful charger, has been crowned prince of the tournament. And in the best medieval tradition, he stands on a raised platform, clutching his helmet, and a wreath of roses is placed around his shoulders while a prince, government officer or celebrity presses a silver trophy in his hands and his country's national anthem is played over the public address system just for him.

The crowd pushes toward him eager to view the hero of the day. Autograph hunters thrust programs and scraps of paper at him. He is protected by a police guard. His name is shouted reverently by throngs. Newspapers and magazines feature stories about his win. Girls want to touch him. Eminent persons seek him out. In Europe he is accepted on the highest social levels. Everywhere he wanders, he is recognized as a superior being, one who laughs in the face of danger, one who experiences no timidity, no apprehension. He observes envy in the eyes of the average race fan, who views him as a bold, gallant, modern Red Baron.

Psychologically, the driver is not a nine-to-five person. Fiercely independent and dedicated to his own ideals, he places immense value on his personal liberty. He enjoys doing what he chooses when he chooses. Working only on weekends is pleasant indeed. Not much time is required from his fascinating life of gay parties, lovely girls and new countries.

A driver here or there will tell you that he is not interested in gay parties, lovely girls and new countries. But then some people will tell you anything.

The driver is a cocksure person. Though most of the time this confidence is covered by a thin patina of shyness, he believes in himself totally. But then, he must. Split-second decisions are demanded at 200 mph. Uncertainty could be fatal. This positive attitude, a form of conceit, is as essential in racing as it is in bull-fighting. Some time ago an annoyed reporter asked a famous bullfighter why he had to be so damn conceited. The bullfighter replied, "It is an occupational necessity, my friend. If I don't believe in myself, the bull certainly won't believe in me." A driver must believe in his abilities to control the car, or the car will destroy him.

In the last analysis, the glamour, the adulation, the high speeds and the possibility of being king of the world for a weekend are the things that hook men, both young and old, on motor racing. It's a fever few can shake once it gets in the blood. Rare is the driver who retires before he is forced to. Drivers remain on the track until they are carried from it or until they become excessively cautious and can't beg a ride any longer.

Going against the trend, Hans Herrmann gave a demonstration of clear thinking by deciding to quit at the age of forty-two—an age when reflexes slow up.

Herrmann, Attwood, Siffert, Rodriguez—these were

the men for the 917s, the star drivers of the Salzburg and Wyer teams. Herrmann and Attwood would try one approach. Siffert and Rodriguez would try another. Both were valid techniques by brave men. Men different from the crowd.

These drivers were ready to race. The Porsche 917 was ready. And so was the opposition. The battle for Le Mans would be monumental.

11 | The Enemy

Chief competition for the 917 at Le Mans was provided by Ferrari, Matra and Alfa Romeo. Of the three marques, Ferrari was the most seriously regarded. The Ferraris were traditionally durable cars with sound engines. They didn't fall apart bit by bit during a race as did the cars of some constructors. Ferrari engineers emphasized body solidity. Over and over, Ferrari sacrificed weight reduction for strength. And strength was the secret for victory at Le Mans.

Le Mans was the Ferrari "home track." Or so it seemed. Ferrari victory seemed to follow Ferrari victory on the Sarthe circuit. True, the Fords did dominate the scene for a while. But they went back to the States, forever. Ferrari never left. Enzo Ferrari considered every year at Le Mans to be *his* year. During one winning streak, his cars won the race six years in a row!

If the Porsche people had a car to fear, if they had a deadly enemy in their struggle for victory at Le Mans, it had to be Ferrari.

Ferraris have been feared on the racetracks of the world for many years. Their string of victories is fantastic. Why? Because the blood-red cars are virtually the extensions of the personality of the man who creates them: Enzo Ferrari.

In his sixties, Enzo is severe, aloof, frightening. He has assumed the bearing and manner of an old-line aristocrat. Associates and employees never sit when he is standing. They even seem ready to bow. Without question they are nervous in his awesome presence. The old auto maker even has a title—*Commendatore*—that was bestowed upon him by the Italian king as a tribute for the honor he brought Italy.

Enzo Ferrari has traveled a long road to the rank of Commendatore. He started his career as a blacksmith in the Italian army during World War I. Perhaps he was an aristocratic blacksmith. Attitudes towards life and people seldom change. Aristocratic, stern old men begin life as aristocratic, stern children. Later he became an aristocratic racing driver. In 1925 he was named racing manager of Alfa Romeo. Subsequently he purchased the team cars, formed his own racing group under his own name and began to achieve considerable fame and a modest fortune.

His ambition was to field a team of cars of his own design. In 1939 he opened a factory in Modena to construct what he hoped would be championship-caliber racing cars. He had his own ideas of how a car should be designed. Strong ideas. Certain stubborn men wouldn't listen to him. He would do it himself. He *knew* his ideas were sound.

Then the bad guys pressed the red button, starting World War II. Ferrari picked up his machines and walked ten miles down the road to Maranello, where he felt his equipment wouldn't be hit by stray bombs or bullets. During the war, he made tools.

The all-new Ferrari cars appeared almost on the day the war ended. Enzo had prepared. He had prepared to win races. He did win. Ferrari cars have been the most successful racing vehicles of all time. What's more, Enzo has made good money in racing when most manufacturers consider themselves lucky if they break even. No one has ever accused the old man of being less than a genius in the engineering and business departments.

Racing is his life, and he puts in fifteen hours a day, seven days a week. The rest of the world is separated from him by a thick veil of oblivion. Entertainment and frivolity represent extravagant waste. Work is virtue to him.

Drivers have confidence in the Italian cars for two reasons: 1) they know that the suspension system won't snap into pieces on turn one; 2) they feel that the tough body will protect them in case of an accident. Believing in a car and feeling safe in a car enable a driver to push beyond his normal limits, thus securing the laurel wreath when everyone else knows victory is *not* within the province of the particular car/driver combination.

Unlike the bright, airy Porsche factory, the Ferrari works are somber, forbidding, encircled by a high fence—a virtual fortress guarded by uniformed men and requiring a pass for admittance. Here with his three hundred employees Enzo Ferrari produces cars that win races.

In 1970 he was determined to capture the trophy at Le Mans. Ford had broken his winning streak. The Americans had snatched his crown as "King of Le Mans." Now the Germans were coming after him.

Well, he had fought Germans before. They could be beaten. He accepted the challenge.

With a characteristic burst of speed, Ferrari and his engineers designed the 512 to combat the Porsche 917.

The Commendatore first talked business (support money?) with Fiat. After that, the new Le Mans 512 project flew together. Ferrari had years of experience with big endurance cars. Where Porsche needed development time, Ferrari simply needed assembly time.

The 512 engine was based on an old Ferrari workhorse design. In fact, old castings were used. The Can-Am 6.9-litre engine was reduced to a 4994-cc capacity. In practice, when an engine is stretched, it loses some of its durability. Conversely, when the cylinder capacity is reduced, it should increase in strength. The percentage of failure should decrease. The 512's heart should be extra strong.

The Porsche and the Ferrari engines had many matching muscles. Both had 12 cylinders. At one point in development both punched out 560 bhp at 8500 rpm. The basic Ferrari engine was lighter than the 917 unit, but the Porsche engine included a cooling system.

Set in a 60-degree vee design with four camshafts, the Ferrari 512 engine could, in emergencies, be revved to 9600 rpm without harm! Now that's *tough*. That is the kind of strength Ferrari has forged a lasting reputation on.

The tough engine was positioned in a tough chassis. Steel tubing ran back and forth, over and under, imitating a giant spider web. Sheet aluminum was tightly wrapped around the center section and riveted. The construction was heavy, but it was strong. More meat for the Ferrari reputation.

Unlike Porsche, which cools its engines by air,

Ferrari employs the traditional water-cooling method requiring radiators. These radiators were mounted on the sides of the 512 body in front of the rear tires.

In addition to being noted for their strength, Ferraris are famous for their beauty. You'll never see an ugly Ferrari. Perhaps the reason is that they come from the land of Leonardo Da Vinci, Michelangelo and warm, dark-eyed ladies. Everything the Italians do is steeped in high drama and pure art. They wave their hands in conversation. They pinch the bottoms of young ladies who walk past them. They create magnificent statues. They paint unequaled frescoes. They build imposing monuments. They design exciting clothes. And sometimes they shoot those who disagree with them. Italians have style.

This style was displayed in the 512, a self-propelled piece of sculpture. Smooth and sleek, it was an exercise in aerodynamic design. Harmony and grace were exhibited in its curving profile. Watching it perform was an emotional experience.

In the manner of artists everywhere, Enzo Ferrari was not satisfied with the shape of his creation after it was first introduced (at Daytona). The second time the 512 was seen—six weeks later at Sebring—the car's nose had been bobbed and the tail had been lifted. The sculptor was at work perfecting his masterpiece. He stirred the innards around a bit, too, effecting a higher top speed than the Porsche 917 produced.

The 512 was now ready to battle the 917. It would be the clash of the century. David and Goliath once again. An upstart against the old champion. The rugged north against the refined south. The battlefield was the jousting fields of Le Mans. The prize: the respect of the world and a barrel of money from the many sales of street cars that are inevitably sparked by the Big Win.

The Porsche 917 was fast, light, reliable, but volatile. By comparison, the Ferrari 512 was faster, heavier by some 200 pounds, sluggish in turns, predictable and plagued with minor ailments. A good match.

Ickx, Parks, Posey, Andretti and even the new American superstar Mark Donohue would drive Ferraris in the great contest with Porsche. These were typical Ferrari pilots—fierce men with fire in their eyes. The timid, or those who choose to give less than all, need not apply.

The Porsche platoon of drivers was brillant, also. Herrmann, Attwood, Rodriguez and Siffert were at the top of the list of sportscar drivers.

The battle lines were drawn. Ferrari vs. Porsche. Veteran campaigner of big cars vs. the newcomer. 512 vs. 917. Winner take Le Mans.

12 | The Car Doctors Examine the 917

Engineers conceive and design a car, but mechanics keep it moving, keep it competitive. They nurse it. They baby it. They take it apart and put it back together again . . . and again . . . and again. These men actually breathe life into a car's copper veins. They attempt to squeeze a little more speed, greater ease in handling and guaranteed start-to-finish endurance from the designer's blue-sky dream. These men with grease-smeared clothes, smudgy faces, scratched hands and dirty fingernails are vital to the success of any racing car.

Before a race begins the mechanics check the total vehicle. During the race they often reassemble the car. After a race they examine it and replace worn or damaged parts. They know their team's cars. Inside out. And they know the opposition's cars as well, since many mechanics switch from team to team. It's a job with Porsche this year, Ferrari next year. They know which cars are structurally superior. Drivers and team managers respect their judgment and in fact rely upon their opinions in forming key decisions.

What do the mechanics think of the 917? How do the men who eat and sleep with this racing rascal regard him?

And what are the mechanics themselves like? Let's take a look at these men and get their opinions.

First of all let's meet Porsche's Hermann Briem and tour his department with him. Let's look in the cracks and corners of the Porsche racing department.

Briem is a man who knows the 917 as well as anyone. Head of the racing repair department at Porsche, he has supervised the construction and reconstruction of 917s from the beginning.

A stocky man of average height, Briem is extremely knowledgeable about all Porsche cars—not especially surprising in view of his official position and the fact that he has been a Porsche mechanic or mechanic supervisor for over twenty years.

He, like most other Porsche employees, has a warm regard for the company that has fed and clothed him. He is proud of the 10,000 square feet of machinery, men and equipment that comprise his department. "We have fifty dynos here," he said as he rapidly ripped off a verbal inventory. "Some of them are equipped with electric counting systems to check gas flow." He smiled as he surveyed his domain.

Walking down the narrow aisles where mechanics were meticulously reconditioning 917 and 908 engines, he added, "We do a little machine work here. And we grind brake drums as well as repair discs, cylinder heads and valve guides. We're versatile."

The repair shop reflected the antiseptic and tidy conditions usually associated with German craftsmanship.

Mechanics wore spotless long white frocks. Floors were scrubbed to a shine. Not a grease smear anywhere. Men were stationed in geometric patterns. Shiny metal parts waiting to be repaired resembled a neat display of modern sculpture. Men hovered over complex and intricate machinery that seemed to demand the care of a watch repairman rather than a mechanic. Chatter and gossip were not heard. Everyone was busy with his task and seemed to enjoy his job. Morale was high. So was quality of workmanship. Order and discipline were striking characteristics of the department.

Briem knows each of his fifty men by name, and he knows their jobs, too. He is a boss of the old school, who believes he should be capable of completing most assignments as skillfully as the men who are actually doing them. Knowledge is important in his book. "You don't fake anything if you expect to succeed."

He leaned on the door to his wire-mesh-enclosed office. Scratching his head of graying hair he said, "Oh, we do simple jobs here, too. We'll look at your car even if you aren't a racing driver. An eighty-year-old lady regularly brings her car here to be repaired. We drive it fast on the highway, blowing out the bad stuff, and return it to her in perfect shape. She never drives over 35 miles per hour, so it gets sticky."

He picked up a technical manual and patted it. "We're also involved in training. If you want to start your own Porsche racing team, we'll train your mechanics. Free of charge. They'll work side by side with my boys and really learn the insides of a 917. They'll know what it's all about before they leave here. Believe me."

Walking towards the outside double door, he said, "We repair the bodies in that building over there." He pointed down the driveway. "Let's take a look. . . ."

"Private racing teams from all over the world send their cars here to be rebuilt or repaired. Cars have been shipped from as far away as Japan."

Cars in various states of agony were carefully arranged around the body shop. There were cars with obscenely ripped bodies, and cars without wheels, cars with grimly shattered windscreens. All racing accidents.

What had happened to the drivers? "This one had a broken leg. That one three cracked ribs. And he . . . well, he was unhurt. Unbelievable!"

Briem smiled warmly. "We receive some surprising requests. The owner of a Ferrari ordered a 917 windscreen. He felt it resisted shock to a high degree. Another Ferrari owner is running on Porsche wheels. He says they are better–and less expensive. We'll sell parts to almost anyone. We don't object."

He walked into a courtyard driveway. Cars for which you would happily commit murder were parked around the outer borders. The sun sparkled on 911s, 914/6s and warmly caressed a sleeping 917.

Walking to the low-slung champion, Briem said, "Now here's a car. I've been with Porsche for over twenty years and I think that this is the best yet. Look at it!"

He slowly walked around the 917, smiling possessively the way a mother smiles at her child.

Then he looked up, "The engine is the factor that has contributed most to the 917's success. It is big. Strong. Rugged. And it is air-cooled, which eliminates some potential trouble. No radiator or overheating problems. Every problem that you do not eliminate means a race that you will not win."

He walked around the 917 again. His eyes twinkled.

"An excellent automobile. My boys love to work on the engine. It is complex, but at the same time it is simple. The design is superb, intelligent, logical. Although it is a twelve-cylinder engine, my boys prefer it to the four-cylinder Carrera. The engine is easy, from a mechanic's viewpoint. Yes, it is easy to work on, and it is easy to learn."

Briem started walking back to the repair shop. "The brakes are excellent. We had some early trouble. Now we have no difficulties with them."

In the shop he picked a brake cylinder from a bin. "See this?" he asked. "The vents and random holes assist in cooling and they also eliminate weight. Mice have not been in here nibbling, even if these brakes do resemble Swiss cheese."

Briem walked over to an engine. He was a man who was in his element. He loved his work. And it showed in his warm, slow-talking, easy-does-it personality. His calm manner, interlaced with his crisp intelligence and joy-in-living attitude, propelled him up to this important spot at Porsche. These same characteristics would have carried him to any position of his choosing. He knows his job. And he knows the 917.

"You may consider this odd," he said as he picked up an air-cooling fan, "but some parts of this 917 engine are made of plastic! The reason is weight. Racing cars must be as light as possible. As you know, plastic is lighter than metal. Porsche has been successfully using plastic for ten years."

Briem shuffled his feet in embarrassment. "You know, I was the first Porsche racing mechanic. Way back in 1951. Those were the days. Believe me, Porsche wasn't the large company it is now. But we would win races. In class, of course. I worked many races, but usually I was assigned the job of racing mechanic at Le Mans. Now there's an exciting race. A *real* race. Twenty-four hours of torture. And it was won this year at long last by a Porsche. Without question, the winning 917 is the greatest racing car to hit the tracks. I know. I've seen a lot of cars in my time."

In the mid-1950s, Briem represented Porsche in the United States, where he prepared actor Steve McQueen's car (a Porsche, strangely enough) for races in California.

Briem said, "After losing contact with McQueen for several years, I ran into him when he was filming *Le Mans*. McQueen thought I had gotten older. And you know, I have."

Every mechanic uses a slightly different yardstick to measure the qualities of the 917. Let's examine a few other viewpoints.

Hugo Schibler, personal mechanic for the late Jo Siffert, said, "The 917 is a great car. It is hard. It is fast. Most important of all it holds together. If a car is fast and it falls apart before the race ends, the speed is meaningless. The car is worthless. Speed in itself is nothing. Nothing. Endurance is everything. I have seen slow cars win races because the ultrafast, ultralight, ultrafragile cars started to lose bits and pieces on the first lap. By the twenty-fifth lap the driver was lucky to have the steering wheel connected."

Schibler crawled under Siffert's Can-Am 917. "You know, this 917 is not the same as the Le Mans 917. This is an open car. The Le Mans car is closed. This is short and squat. The Le Mans car is long and graceful. Even the short-tail version of the Le Mans car is longer and less boxy than this. Engine and suspension setups differ, also. The Le Mans 917 is an endurance car constructed to win long-distance races under World Championship Series rules. The Can-Am car competes in short two-hour sprint races. The design, mechanical requirements, as well as the series rules, differ. So, in effect, the Le Mans 917 and the Can-Am 917 are two completely different cars."

He pulled his thin frame from under the blunt-nosed vehicle. "No problems under there. Seldom are any."

Neatly stacking his gleaming tools in a red metal box, Schibler said, "The 917 is complicated. Some do not agree with me. But I say it is a more difficult car to work on than its predecessor, the 908. But then, it is superior to the 908. So it should be more complex."

He picked up a soft rag and wiped the grease off each finger. Then he continued, "In different races I look for different problems with the 917. At Sebring I worry about the brakes and chassis. At the Nurburgring the transmission, suspension and the chassis receive my special care. At Le Mans, I sweat over the engine. After twenty-four hours the engine really has taken a beating. I'd hate to have to run at two hundred and thirty miles per hour for twenty-four hours. My insides would surely break. Poor car."

Schibler knows his Porsches. A young man with eight years' experience, he was trained as a mechanic at the Porsche works at Stuttgart and subsequently worked there. Later Siffert asked him to become his personal racing mechanic. Being a racing mechanic is the dream of most young men who do auto surgery. Schibler is no exception. Eagerly he accepted the offer. A dream job with a top driver! Life can be sweet!

Without question, Schibler is a master at his trade. Siffert selected him for his skill, competence and thoroughness. In auto racing, a mechanic's reputation goes before him like a scent blown by a soft wind. Siffert liked the reputation.

A driver must have confidence in his mechanic. The job of a racing mechanic involves more than spinning wrenches and inflating tires. The mechanic literally holds the driver's life in his hands. If the mechanic forgets to inspect all components previous to a race, or if he doesn't bother to fully tighten a single little nut, the driver may die in an explosive crash. Of course, the driver may crash and burn and perhaps die due to accidental mechanical failure anyway. But that is an occupational hazard which the driver accepts, lives with and doesn't think about. Accidents will happen and that's that. Every driver knows this. He knows how Jimmy Clark died. And how Bruce McLaren died. And how Jochen Rindt died. If he were afraid of accidents he would take a job testing overstuffed mattresses. Something soft, comfortable, without a challenge. However, a driver thrives on challenge and competition. The possibility of partaking in a tire-screaming, spinning, fiery accident is stuffed into the darkest, smallest cubbyhole in his mind. A driver who dwells on, entertains or seriously considers the probability of a mechanical breakdown in his next race will not drive in a competitive manner in that race. He'll fall behind. He won't push. He'll gently ease around the corners, instead of sliding in a rush through them. He won't approach the car in front of him too closely. (If something gave way, both of them would be demolished.) He carefully watches trees, and curbs and telephone poles, and concrete retaining walls—all nasty obstacles that stop race cars rather suddenly. Rapidly he is transformed from a racing driver to a man who drives in races. When this happens, his career nosedives into a pool of murky oil and he disappears from the racing world.

Another racing mechanic who has traveled with Porsche to all the tracks of the world for many years said, "Of course the car is good. Why shouldn't it be good? It's expensive enough. It would cost you $70,000 to buy a Le Mans 917. You could buy a squadron of Volkswagens for that money. The engine alone runs approximately $35,000. Everything about the 917 is expensive. The crankshaft costs $2500. The oil cooler: $300; gas tanks: $1500; unibolt: $70; clutch: $700. Even the job of replacing twenty-four sparkplugs runs into high numbers. To be exact: $700. This is not a cheap automobile. No competitive racing car is cheap these days. Big money went into the development of the 917 and it takes big money to buy one. During 1970 and 1971, the 917 coupe was *the* car to own if you wanted to be competitive in endurance racing. There was no other. Porsche won. The other makes got exercise. If a car wins, the cost can be excused. Everyone looks at the win-loss column anyway. In years to come people will ask, 'Did it win?' Not 'How much did it cost?' Feel sorry for those who bought Ferraris during 1970 and 1971. They didn't win. Ferraris are also expensive, you know."

Not all mechanics sing elaborate songs of praise to the 917. Men servicing non-Porsche teams are sharply critical of the cars from Stuttgart. Upon analyzing their comments, it becomes apparent that these mechanics are not necessarily down on the 917, but rather they disagree with the Porsche concept of building automobiles. Air-cooled engines meet with disfavor in many quarters. So do the Porsche chassis and suspension systems. Nothing is loved by all the people all the time.

François Sicard, the chief mechanic on the Gregg Young Ferrari team, said, "The 917 is a tough car. It stays together. Nevertheless, I prefer the Ferrari."

Sicard has solid experience in racing. He has been a mechanic for former World Champion Graham Hill, and he has worked for such teams as Matra and Mercedes.

"The Porsche is not so interesting as the Ferrari," he said. "The gearbox on the Ferrari is simple. Simplicity is a key element in racing. Complexity means breakdowns. In my opinion the Ferrari's chassis geometry is superior, also. And I prefer the Ferrari clutch system. I guess I'm just partial to Ferraris. Although I've worked on Porsches during my career, I was never entranced by them. Perhaps I'm the exception."

These are the comments of the car doctors–the mechanics. Like medical doctors, they spend long hours with their patients, preparing them for their place in life. With a knowledge of the intricate mechanical viscera and capricious attitudes of their charges, these men must be acknowledged as possessing special vision in the nuts-and-bolts, get-'em-to-go, practical side of racing.

And get 'em to go they do. Come what may. More often than a racing mechanic likes to remember, a team driver has turned a car into a pretzel on the day before the race. The good mechanic then has his duty outlined for him. In the time-honored tradition of good British soldiers, the good mechanic (any nationality) will never ask why; he will just go without sleep for twenty-four or more hours to untangle the scramble created by an overeager driver who has read Stirling Moss's biography too frequently. And the car will be in racing condition the next afternoon.

During the racing season, sleep actually becomes a rare and precious luxury for most mechanics. An engine must be replaced or repaired, brakes must be changed, this must be straightened, that must be pounded out. Deadlines are firm. The race will start at the appointed time, come what may.

And once again the mechanic is straining at a stubborn bolt under a naked light bulb in a dark corner of a damp and drafty rented garage in the middle of a deserted track. Bright-eyed drivers are dancing with lively blondes. Team managers are resting in comfortable hotel rooms. The clock ticks on and soon they are all asleep—drivers, blondes, and team managers.

Night reaches the hollow hours when the world seems to be empty. Dark silence echoes faintly across broad plains and lonely race circuits. But wait. Someone remains awake. The naked light bulb is still burning. The mechanic is still bent over the skeleton of the car, attempting to breathe life into it. Now his eyes are bloodshot and almost glowing in the dark. His back feels as if it has been whipped with hooks. His feet must be three yards wide. He hasn't fallen over yet. In spite of his personal agony and the impossible conditions, the car will be ready for the race in the morning. No member of the team ever doubted that. Not the driver. Not the team manager. Not the clever young ladies who loiter in the pits.

Is he paid in bags of gold for his superhuman efforts? No. He earns $100 a week if he is a journeyman. Without question, he could earn more at the corner garage.

But that could be boring—life without a challenge. The racing mechanic lives for challenge in much the same manner as the driver. Life must be a glass of bubbly champagne to these men. Not sour beer. They love their jobs. The same faces appear at the tracks year after year after year. The lure of competition has hooked them . . . permanently. Nobody drops out.

Many of them stick with racing because they enjoy traveling—with all expenses paid. The United States, France, England, Austria, Germany and Italy are countries they visit annually. Be a racing mechanic and see the world.

Complaints have been heard about poor hotels, poor food and poor companions. Yet nobody is serious in his criticisms. Nobody drops out of the sportscar carnival. To complain is human.

The only persons who seriously howl about conditions caused by the traveling racing troop are the wives and girl friends who have been left behind.

During the few weeks the mechanic is at home, the good woman generally works him over verbally. But before the mechanic can reconsider his career, he is safely off to the races again—beyond the range of her screams.

Usually two mechanics are assigned to a car, with one man in charge. In this manner they rapidly learn a particular car and the setups required by the car's driver. The two-mechanics-one-car unit is the basis of the modern racing team. Found efficient, practical and speedy, this system is being adapted on an international scale.

Responsibility. This is the outstanding characteristic of racing mechanics. They rebuild a car on schedule only to see it demolished in short order. Aware that they hold a driver's life in their hands, they examine every nut, bolt, tube and weld of a car before every race. Life is precious. The responsibility is monumental.

And the vast majority of these professionals said that the Le Mans 917 was the greatest racer of its time. They should know.

usual things occur. No one knows what will happen during a day and a night of racing at speeds ranging to 230 mph. The components of racing cars behave strangely at times. The components of racing drivers behave more strangely still.

The 917 had been tested and tested and tested. Porsche executives had hand-picked two teams to lead the assault on Le Mans. Drivers had been selected with equal care. Race fans would see the 917s handled in contrasting driving techniques. Wyer team members were "chargers." Salzburg pilots believed in conserving the machinery.

The big car was ready to go. Engineers had smoothed its rougher edges. Mechanics had examined it and declared it a winner.

Opposition was ready to go also. The 512s that arrived at Le Mans were a little more refined, a little more sophisticated than they were earlier in the season. The rear tires were one inch wider. Velocity stacks were new. Intake porting was changed as well as the cam. Some 512s appeared with a sweeping long tail and fins. Old Enzo was applying all the knowledge he had acquired from six Le Mans victories. He was determined to give Porsche a fast run for the money.

Matra had prepared for Le Mans, also. This team deliberately missed several races to get primed up for the big one. Matra brought in one new 660 and two 650s. The 660 was sleeker in design than its predecessors. Innovations consisted of a new suspension system and a monocoque body that stopped ahead of the engine. Lighter and less complex than the 650, the new car was, nonetheless, slower. In spite of this shortcoming, Matra was able to sign on first-class talent. Jean-Pierre Beltoise and Henri Pescarolo were given the new 660. Former

World Champion Jack Brabham/François Cevert and Jean-Pierre Jabouille/Patrick Depailler were the pairings for the 650s.

Alfa Romeo entered four beautiful 33–3s. Long-tailed with fins, the Alfas were exquisitely finished. Their position in the race was unimportant to the spectators; they were just a delight to look at. (Of course, position was important to Alfa.)

Although the race was set for Saturday, the track area was the scene of a whirlpool of activity during the entire preceding week. Teams arrived from all over the world in rapid succession. Immense vans the size of railroad cars chugged down narrow rural roads, negotiating tight curves, looking like fat old ladies trying to balance on a curbstone. The vans entered the racetrack vicinity, searched for their predesignated resting spots, found them, then jerked four feet forward, six feet backward, four feet forward and shuddered to a stop. Steel ramps were lowered and shiny racing cars were eased out of the vans' huge bellies. Ferraris here Alfas there. Porsches farther down the line.

Some of the teams headed to garages in the vicinity of Le Mans, where they established their working areas. Other teams went to the track first.

Until the vans with their expensive cargo arrived, the Le Mans track resembled a country fairground in Indiana. Now, there could be no confusing the scene. Immense vans at rest, sleek race cars being prepared, confident drivers strutting, tired mechanics dragging and the screams of revving engines marked the site as an auto race of international importance.

Porsche factory representatives arrived at Le Mans early in the week of the race, establishing their headquarters in their usual garage beyond Mulsanne Straight.

Not wanting to be caught short, they brought with them an extraordinary amount of tools and spare parts—almost enough equipment and bits and pieces to repair all automotive vehicles used by the Germans in World War II. Porsche people weren't taking any chances. Races have been lost for want of a $1.95 replacement part. Tires, wheels, shock absorbers, springs, torsion bars, transmission components, doors, windscreens, batteries, alternators and strong German coffee were stacked in towering columns waiting for a series of disasters to strike. Porsche had taken the count in the last round at Le Mans in 1969. They wanted to win by a knockout before they got punchy. They were prepared. There was probably even a kitchen sink in the pile of parts. (You never know what you might need.)

Sleeping accommodations were rare in the Le Mans area. Even persons involved with the race had trouble finding rooms. The Wyer team was billeted in Chartres, roughly a hundred miles from Le Mans.

Richard Attwood and his lovely wife Veronica had a hotel reservation, only to discover that the hotel was a disaster and the room was worse. Checking out almost before they checked in, they phoned the Wyer group for help. Quickly accommodations were procured in Wyer's hotel.

Hans Herrmann stayed with old friends in a private home, as was his custom.

On Tuesday the fifty-one cars entered in the race were examined by officials and affixed with seals. The French place great value on examinations, rules, regulations and officialdom.

At Le Mans persons with unrelated vocations are selected as "official inspectors." This race provides the butcher and the baker an opportunity to play Great Bureaucrat for a day. They examine and examine and examine, and the day grows hotter and hotter and hotter. Occasionally tempers grow short.

This technical inspection can be quite a sideshow. Most mechanics don't speak French. French tech inspectors believe that they will befoul their mouths if they speak anything other than French. Fifteen-minute-long dissertations in French have been given in great style and flourish when the orator knew perfectly well that he wasn't being understood. He might as well have been speaking in ancient Babylonian. Tech inspections generate the trust and harmony found at the Paris peace talks.

The inspectors were positioned at little tables, with each table being assigned a specialty, such as headlights, suspensions, fuel systems, etc.

When an inspector could not make a decision, he huddled with his compatriots and they discussed the predicament in machine-gun French, which sounded like a secret code to the uninitiated. More suspicion.

Resembling a combination of an oriental bazaar and hog auction, the inspection drew a vast audience. Journalists, photographers, film crews and spectators filled the three-sided shed so tightly that those who had business there had difficulty conducting it.

Fortunately for the tempers of all involved, the 917s passed inspection without a major confrontation. The harangues, threats and counterthreats of 1969 were not repeated.

On Tuesday afternoon, Herrmann, Attwood and all the other drivers were given medical examinations in the clinic tent. Standing in line with their shirts off, the drivers cracked jokes or stood in moody silence.

Length of service at Le Mans determined their attitudes. Youngsters with no time on the track were usually struck dumb by the rich tradition and history of the event. The veterans had been everywhere, seen everything and run in everything. Nothing intimidated them, although they good-naturedly attempted to psych each other.

"Driving a Porsche 917 this round?"

"Yes. And what a car it is!"

"Be careful *it* doesn't drive *you.* I heard they are man-eaters."

"No. Just Ferrari-eaters."

In a race as important as Le Mans, constructors leave as little as possible to chance. Before the Wyer and the Salzburg teams arrived at the track, the Porsche firm had attempted to provide as much insurance as possible. Facts and figures were fed into a computer. Yes, the omnipresent computer is employed to influence the outcome of auto races. No facet of existence is safe from the menacing expertise of the mechanical brain—not even something as personal and emotion-charged as auto racing. A glut of information was shoveled into the computer's mouth. Out of its ear came a long sheet with the 917's every shift point charted, a map of the course, five gear ratios for peak torque at optimum rev range, engine rpm for every significant point on the course and more. The computer's innards buzzed and glowed, but they did produce.

The computer did not, however, provide all the answers. During the first practice sessions, the 917s were extremely jumpy on the straights. An old problem recurring? No. Just an old difficulty caused by a new situation. After much head-scratching, it was discovered that the tires were leaking air upon acceleration. The rims were quickly modified and the problem solved.

Although both the Wyer team and the Salzburg team had access to the same information, their cars were not identical. On the short-tail 917, each team preferred a different, rear-flap construction. The Wyer team retained the flap in the original position as it was fabricated during the testing session at Zeltweg; the flap, angled up, connected the two box fenders in the middle of the car at the rear. The Salzburg team eliminated the middle flap altogether. To achieve the downthrust, they turned up the trailing edge of each rear fender.

To improve the durability and balance of the 917, Wyer also reinforced the body and framework. Since the light body work seemed determined to fly to pieces upon contact with solid objects, such as steel guardrails and concrete embankments, he felt that additional metal tubes would provide a safer vehicle for his low-flying pilots.

And they would be flying. Porsche had juiced up the engines. Now 4.9-litre power plants producing 600 hp at 8400 rpm were available to the teams. These larger engines were designed specifically to combat the threat posed by the 5-litre Ferrari 512s. Initially, Porsche engineers had calculated that the top speed of the bigger 917 engine would be 240, but drag factors reduced this figure. However, at 230, the 917s weren't exactly crawling.

The 917 came in various colors as well as engine sizes. Traditionally, color schemes in auto racing were conservative and nationalistic. English teams painted their cars deep green. Italian cars glowed a vivid red. Frenchmen raced blue cars. The German color was white. Usually the colors were solid with a white or yellow stripe. The Wyer Porsches normally would have been green. However, Gulf oil supplied the finances and

Gulf executives thought that the Gulf colors would be fitting hues for their cars. Gulf "old school" colors are blue and orange. Gulf Wyer Porsches were blue and orange. Even the giant Mercedes transporter used by the Wyer team was painted blue and orange. Not to be outdone, Anatole Lapine of the Porsche design studio produced unique, even startling, color schemes for two 917s. The Herrmann/Attwood car was painted in orange and white horizontal stripes while the Larrousse/Kauhsen Martini 917 was decorated in purple and green swirls! Some persons loved this Disneyland touch. The British press considered it in bad taste. At the very least it was an injection of high spirits into European inflexibility.

Richard Attwood requested the old 4.5-litre version of the 917 for his ride. The engine was proven and the car was proven. "Le Mans is no place for experimentation if you want to win," he said. Attwood didn't want to gamble on unknown problems of stress, strain and fuel consumption. (The latter point turned out to be of no significance.)

As June approached, he had second thoughts about the 4.5 engine. Top speed became increasingly important in his mind. He decided that the 4.5 wouldn't be quick enough to match the 4.9 Porsches or the big Ferraris. But he remained with the 4.5-litre 917 anyway.

Since practice at Le Mans is limited to two evening sessions starting at 6 P.M. on Wednesday and Thursday, and time on the track is extremely limited in any case, some teams sneak in practice time on public roads.

The Salzburg team actually commandeered a gas station to practice refueling. Their pit stops were slower than they considered ideal. Improvement was necessary. Every minute wasted in the pits causes a driver to lose a place to an opponent. Rapid pit stops and Coca Cola are two American exports that are highly respected by Europeans. Nothing went right during this informal practice. During the practice period involving refueling and a driver change, an overeager mechanic closed the door too soon, hitting the driver and knocking him headfirst into the car. That effort was hardly a record-breaking pit stop. Try it once again, boys.

Wednesday evening Dieter Spoerry, who placed second in 1968, hopped in an old Porsche 908 to run a couple of practice laps. Although he was scheduled to drive a 917 in the race, his big car wasn't ready. He wanted to familiarize himself with the track again, so he just borrowed the smaller Porsche. Getting the feel of the track, he gradually worked up to speed. Traffic was thick. Everyone wanted to sort out his car. Just before the chicane, Spoerry's 908 and an Alfa 650 touched. A touch was enough. The 908 slid across the track, hit an embankment, spun in the opposite direction, hit a rail and bounced back to the embankment. First the transmission broke loose and tore into the earth. Then the car was actually ripped in two pieces. The rear end (with Spoerry strapped in) spun like a top. When it finally came to a halt, Spoerry unbuckled and leaped out. Immediately his part of the car exploded. Fortunately he was lying on the ground, a safe distance from the force of the blast. Unhurt, but suffering from a serious case of the shakes, he was unable to drive in the race. Rico Steinemann, his codriver and team manager, withdrew the entry.

The key practice or training period, which is really the equivalent of American time trials, is conducted on Thursday night. This is the last opportunity to capture a select spot on the grid. Actually, grid position is not critical to the outcome of a twenty-four-hour race. However, certain drivers, for the sake of team prestige and personal reputation, can be counted on for a blazing display of driving skill in an attempt to win pole position.

The Porsche and Piech families were present at the time trials on Thursday, having arrived at Le Mans on Wednesday for a reception at Courtanvaux Castle, near Le Mans, where Dr. Porsche was honored as a "Membre de la Compagnie des Mousquetaires d'Armagnac."

Because Dr. Porsche was in the pits, an element of competition developed between the Wyer and the Salzburg teams. The best time was now a valued prize to *all* Porsche pilots.

Ferrari wasn't going to cooperate, however. Traditionally, Ferraris were fast cars. And Ferrari drivers were the sort of demons who could squeeze a good lap time out of a three-legged duck. And they were moving tonight. (Ferraris. Not ducks.) Big smiles were on the faces of everyone in the Ferrari pits. Their stopwatches were whispering glad tidings.

Then Vic Elford in a 4.9-litre 917 began to move around the circuit in a brisk manner. Ferrari pit-crew members looked up. Soon they looked sad. Even the bright-eyed blondes hovering at the edges of the Ferrari compound seemed to lose their glow.

With a rare blend of wizardry and passion, Elford hurled the metal monster around the track. The gutsy car slid under the footbridge, skidded through the esses, snapped through Tertre Rouge and accelerated down Mulsanne Straight at speeds that track observers had not witnessed before. At the end of the straight, white markers with black figures informed Elford of an approaching sharp right-hand curve: 500 . . . 400 . . . 300. . . . Snapping through the gears, he simultaneously downshifted and braked to a relative standstill. The grandstands, crowds and barriers seemed to rush toward him. In an instant he was through the corner, gearing upwards, stomping the accelerator, feeling his back and head being pushed hard. Blazing on the pavement through the pine forest, he reached Arange faster than he had expected. Down through the gears again. The rear end of the 917 broke loose, but he spun the wheel back and forth and steadied the car, sliding safely through the corner. He was feeling pretty good as he zipped through White House and entered the Grandstand Straight. The double-decker grandstands and the yellow pits flashed past as the 917's headlights cut a hole in the darkness.

Cheers rose from the Porsche contingent.

"He's done it!"

"A new record!"

"Ferrari will never beat *that* time."

"Good old Vic."

"Good old 917."

When Vic Elford pulled into the pits, Gerhard Strasser asked, "How did it handle at those speeds?"

Elford's craggy, perspiring face smiled. "Smoothly. I could do it with one hand."

Smoothly! Had the volatile 917s turned into gentle pussycats? Or did Elford tame his personal tiger? Without a doubt, the credit must be given to Elford, a fierce driver pushed by a personal demon.

The 917s simply weren't all tenderness and whipped cream.

In addition to being a skilled 917 pilot, Elford is an engineer and postmaster of the little town of Clophill in England. Some racing drivers are men of many interests and pursuits.

As it turned out, Elford's quick zip gave him the pole—but barely. He posted 3:19.8. The Ferrari of Vaccarella/Giunti lapped at 3:20.0. Close? Ferraris were fighting hard. As a matter of fact, the first several positions were a thorough Porsche-Ferrari mixture: Siffert/Redman 917—3:21.1; Merzario/Regazzoni, Ferrari—3:21.3; Rodriguez/Kinnunen 917—3:21.9; Ickx/Schetty, Ferrari—3:23.1.

The rivalry was intense. The qualifying times were only split seconds apart. Le Mans 1970 was going to be a hotly fought contest.

Hans Herrmann and Richard Attwood qualified in sixteenth place at 3:32.6. Conservative drivers, they wanted to save their car for the race.

No practice on Friday. It's a day of rest for the drivers. But not for the mechanics and team managers. A twenty-four-hour endurance race means four times as many problems as the standard six-hour sportscar race. Therefore, the prerace preparations and checks are four times as comprehensive. Generally the examinations continue far into the night. Special attention was given to silly little things because races are frequently lost as a result of them. Naturally, major components were not overlooked either. The 917 checklist was staggering. Alternator belts were checked for damage and tension. The exhaust system was checked for cracks. Manifold nuts were tightened. The condition of the motor oil was examined. Hose clips were tightened. Fuel-pump mountings were secured. Starter motor leads were secured. The transmission casing was examined for cracks. Transmission oil level was checked and double-checked. Stub-axle step-down bolts were tightened and secured with Loctite, and grease was applied under bolt heads.

And so it went. The 917s underwent a comprehensive physical examination that would put most M.D.s to shame. By Saturday morning they were as ready as they would ever be. Healthy, with bright shiny headlights.

The stage was set. Tomorrow the curtain would rise on a drama of speed.

14 | Race Day

The Porsche-Ferrari contest had received thorough coverage in the world's press. Word was out: Porsche *wanted* this one. A heated contest was expected. Thousands of spectators joined the caravan to Le Mans early Saturday morning. They wanted to be present when the fiber glass exploded. In Europe, motor racing is more popular than sex—and leaves everyone just as breathless.

Traffic was a bumper-to-bumper parade that generated many familiar four-letter words.

In each car at least one umbrella and two or three raincoats were stored in a corner. Everyone knows that rain falls at Le Mans. That big bright early-morning sun didn't fool anyone.

Rain adds spice and zest to the race. It is a required portion of the spectacle. The spectators anticipate its promise of dark thrills with diabolic delight. The drivers must not have things too easy. Racing for twenty-four solid hours at airplane speeds in heavy traffic does not represent sufficient danger and challenge. A wet track is the barrier that separates the champions from the fainthearted.

At Le Mans on race day, gendarmes and officials were almost as numerous as fans. In some quarters, the French policeman has received a bad name. In contrast, at Le Mans he is courteous, helpful and especially kind to foreigners. Polite and long-suffering, he patiently listens to strangers deliver lengthy speeches in languages he doesn't know, and then—through ESP or some other marvel—he relays understandable directions.

Le Mans hasn't been kind to drivers. Thirteen have been killed during the race or in practice. John Wolfe, Tom Cole, Maréchal, Hery, Lucien Bianchi, Lucky Cassner, Bino Heinz, Marius Mestivier, Roby Weber, Larivière, Mary, Walter Hansgen and Pierre Levegh paid the ultimate price in their pursuit of the god of speed. Some drivers love the course. They believe that the high speeds, the wet track, the extreme length of the course and the duration of the race provide a satisfying test of their skills. Some drivers hate it and won't race there. Some hate it and race anyway.

Hate it or love it, the time for another ride on the celebrated circle of speed had arrived for all the drivers. The Porsche 917 pilots from the Salzburg team would remember this day with special pleasure.

On race day Richard Attwood of the Salzburg team woke up early. Moving to the window of his hotel room, he spread the curtains and looked out.

"How's the weather?" Veronica Attwood asked sleepily.

"Sunny. But don't let that fool you. Purple clouds are

forming on the horizon. It'll rain. Wouldn't be Le Mans without rain."

They dressed quickly and went downstairs to the hotel dining room where several Wyer team members were having breakfast.

"Morning, Attie."

Richard Attwood smiled a shy, crooked smile. "Good morning, fellows."

"Going to take the prize today?"

"Only time will tell."

"I believe you need a bigger engine."

"Perhaps. The 4.5 *is* a bit light compared to your 4.9 or the Ferrari. But Le Mans is an unpredictable race. And it is a long race. I'll tell you who won the race tomorrow at four-oh-five."

Smiles were exchanged, and Attwood and his wife turned their attention to their eggs, toast and tea.

In their hotel—as in all French hotels—an effort had been made to design the dining room to resemble the throne room of the Versailles Palace. Gold leaf, columns, arches and red velvet swirled in a dreary chipped imitation of royal splendor. The French have not accepted the clean lines of functional architecture. Perhaps the Bauhaus style is too German. Perhaps the French love the past with a passion so great that they cannot accept the present.

After breakfast the Attwoods returned to their rooms, where Richard collected his gear, and together they left for the track.

"We didn't leave a moment too soon," Attwood said, whipping past a slower car in the procession to Le Mans. "All the cars in France seem to be on this road."

Ignoring the other cars, Veronica Attwood contemplated the pastoral setting in silence. If she felt any apprehension about the long hours that lay ahead, she did not show it.

Their car sped through the gently rolling French countryside, making good time in spite of the traffic.

In the immediate vicinity of the track they were forced to slow to a crawling pace. Cars were everywhere, going in all directions. Some cars were attempting to pass on the road apron. Chaos reigned. Police and race officials made valiant attempts to maintain order and keep all vehicles moving in some direction.

Close to the track many persons were walking on the side of the road, carrying camping chairs, umbrellas and bags of food. Recklessly, they would dart between moving cars to cross the road.

More than once Attwood had to jam on the brakes to avoid hitting someone.

Finally Attwood and his wife reached the pit building, showed the proper passes and gained entrance to the track.

At the team trailer Attwood changed into his driving gear. First he donned fire-resistant underwear and then a fire-resistant outer one-piece suit that gripped tightly at the wrists and the ankles. A white fire mask hung loosely around his neck. (Later he would pull it up under his eyes.) Then he slipped his feet into special shoes lined with a fire-resistant material. He pulled on his driving gloves, clenched his fist twice, peeled them off and put them in the pocket of his driving suit.

"It's amazing," Attwood commented to his wife, "how these gloves cling to the steering wheel."

"They seem almost sticky," she said.

"I'm glad I don't have to rely on sweaty, slippery palms."

"The gloves are so light. Every time I pick them up to pack them I think I am lifting air."

"Well, they're not designed for heavy combat in a snowball war."

His wife was polishing his goggles.

"Careful, don't scratch them."

"Have I ever scratched them?"

"Well, no," he said.

"Advice. Advice."

The door opened and Hans Herrmann stepped into the trailer.

His face crinkled into a smile, and there was an exchange of hellos. Herrmann dropped his case in a corner. "Well, this is the big day," he said.

"It sure is," Attwood said. "Bigger for you, perhaps, than for the rest of us."

Herrmann ran a hand through his tousled hair and seemed to be lost in his own private thoughts.

Veronica Attwood came over to him and smiled warmly saying, "I wish you the very best of luck, Hans. I really mean it."

"Thank you. You are kind."

There was a long silence, and Veronica took this as her cue to leave, so the men could discuss their race plans. "There's a pot of tea brewing on the hot plate," she said as she left the trailer.

Herrmann changed into his racing gear.

Attwood poured two cups of tea and handed one cup to Herrmann. The men slouched on the couch and sipped the steaming liquid.

Herrmann said, "You might as well relax. The next few hours are going to seem like weeks."

Attwood smiled broadly, nodded. He stared at the

cup he was holding, then looked up at Herrmann. "About strategy. How will we run it? I think you know my views about this race. Le Mans is a long-distance run. It should be planned accordingly. Too many drivers blaze along at top speeds from the beginning as if it were a two-hour Formula I event. And they either blow up or burn out."

Herrmann ran a hand through his hair. "I agree. I agree. Preservation of our 917 is most important. If we break the car on the sixth lap, we do not win the race. Remember, this will be my last Le Mans. I intend to drive sensibly. I'm not going to push anybody out of the way with my fender."

Attwood smiled again. "We both agree. I suggest that we run as quietly as possible until dawn on Sunday. Conserve the car. Baby it and take as little out of it as possible. When the sun comes up and the other cars have been driven into the earth, we make a strong move forward and take the lead."

Herrmann agreed. "My thoughts exactly."

Inside the rough concrete tunnel leading to the pits the sounds from the public address system and the exuberant clamor of the spectators were reduced to a murmur. Naked light bulbs cast streaks of yellow light in the damp shaft.

Attwood put his hand on Herrmann's shoulder. "I'm pleased. For once I'll be running this race as I think it should be run. The way so many top drivers approach this race never ceases to amaze me. With them it is blaze and brake."

They reached the door to the pits, opened it and greeted their teammates. Since Attwood would take the first go, he put in his earplugs immediately. (The unrelenting sound of a screaming engine can spin a driver's brain around and around. It is too much for the naked ear.)

The pits were now clear of unauthorized personnel. Earlier, thousands of spectators had pushed, shoved and pestered in the pit area. They had picked up tools, rolled tires and posed on cars. Wanting to immerse themselves in what they believed racing was all about, they peeked into corners, pondered lap charts and tried to make conversation with disinterested mechanics. An efficient phalanx of police swept them out.

A thunder of applause rolled from the spectator area as winners of past Le Mans races were brought forward. Then the P.A. system started to pour out the national anthems of the countries of the participants.

Attwood stepped out on the pit apron and waved to his wife who was in the box directly above the Porsche pits. Looking up at the sky, he could see the storm clouds patching over the blue expanse. The air was already heavy with humidity. He wiped his forehead with the sleeve of his driving suit.

A mechanic said to him, "Ferrari has entered eleven cars. What do you think of that?"

"I think Enzo wants to win."

The cars were now being rolled out on the grid to positions earned in preliminary time runs. The light cars moved easily and smoothly, requiring very little effort on the part of mechanics, who pushed with one hand on each fender.

Attwood looked affectionately at the orange and white 917 with the number 23 painted on her nose. He pulled up his face mask and slid on his helmet, then started walking in the direction of the car.

The famous Le Mans footrace was now part of the past. No longer did the drivers—at a given signal—dash across the track, leap into their cars and roar away. Considered unsafe by many drivers, the sprint had been abandoned by race organizers. This year fifty-one cars were lined up at sharp angles to the pit straight. Four flags would start the race.

Attwood opened the 917's door and squeezed in. He buckled the seat belt and the shoulder harness. His eyes scanned the instrument panel. Gauges have no secrets, he thought as he flexed his tightly gloved fingers. But the information they conveyed was limited. The driver was the most important gauge of them all. Attwood would soon know all the rest. In his five turns at the wheel during the next twenty-four hours, he would learn all the car's quirks, strengths and weaknesses.

In the pits, scores of officials were taking their places. A *Commissaire de stande* was assigned to each pit. His job was to keep a sharp eye on mechanics and other crew members to make sure nothing was switched on the car that should not be switched according to regulations. Also roving around the pits were flagmen from whom permission was required before a car could pull out of the pits after stops for gas, tires or repairs.

Attwood waited, slouched down in the 917. The seconds ticked away. . . .

In less than a minute the race would begin.

Epilogue

The 917 was created to win the celebrated Le Mans race. It did. And then some. In 1970, as we have seen, the 917 gobbled up Le Mans as well as the World Manufacturers' Championship. It was a year of intense drama and total achievement for Porsche. Beer steins were lifted high and often in Stuttgart during 1970.

Since the Salzburg team had accomplished its purpose —winning Le Mans—it was disbanded at the end of the 1970 season.

But the 917 raced on. The charger from the Black Forest proved to be worth every gold coin spent developing it.

In 1971 the 917 again captured the Le Mans trophy, plus the Manufacturers' Championship. The car was consistent. At Le Mans 1971, van Lennep and Helmut Marko piloted the Porsche that beat Ferrari. They drove for the Martini team, sponsored by Martini-Rossi, the vermouth people.

In 1971, Richard Attwood teamed with Herbert Muller to snag second place at Le Mans, driving, of all things, a Wyer Porsche 917.

The French-controlled FIA started stirring in the rules pot once again. The German Porsche weapon was much too strong. What to do? Limit engine capacities, *naturellement*. So, the heralds blew their trumpets, and the edict reverberated through the halls of auto racing: "For the 1972 season, engine capacities shall be limited to three litres."

With a swoop of the quill, the 4.9-litre 917 was declared illegal.

Once again conferences were called in the Porsche executive suite. "Now what?" they asked themselves. "Do we begin expensive research to create a new three-litre car? Do we repeat the enormous expense of the 917?"

"We have won Le Mans. Twice. We have shown the world that we equal Ferrari, Ford, Alfa Romeo, Matra and the rest of them. I say *no* to the FIA."

"And I say *no*, also."

"But our foundation is built on racing."

"Concentrate on the Can-Am series in the U.S.A. and Canada."

"Yes!"

"It is agreed."

So in 1972 an official Porsche team did not compete at Le Mans or in any of the races that constitute the Manufacturers' Championship. Instead, the firm contracted with the Roger Penske organization to field a team of special 917s in the Can-Am races. Mark Donohue would be the driver. This arrangement was made, incidentally, before Donohue won the 1972 Indianapolis 500.

The new 917s are squat, open cars with turbocharged engines. They share little resemblance visually or mechanically with the great 917 coupes that campaigned in Europe. For all practical purposes, they are different automobiles.

So the roaring 917s of 1970–71 have vanished from the racing world. And time marches on. Hans Herrmann has retired. Attwood quit recently. The Salzburg team is long gone. The Wyer group is fielding a hybrid called a "Mirage." David Yorke has left the Wyer organization to direct a Formula I team. Jo Siffert is dead. Pedro Rodriguez is dead. A glorious era has ended.